Foodie
SNOB

Foodie
SNOB

Kevin Nelson

LP

Guilford, Connecticut

An imprint of Globe Pequot

Distributed by NATIONAL BOOK NETWORK

Illustrations by Meredith Nelson

British Library Cataloguing in Publication Information Available

Library of Congress Cataloging-in-Publication Data
Names: Nelson, Kevin, 1953– author.
Title: Foodie snob / Kevin Nelson.
Description: Guilford , Connecticut : Lyons Press, [2017]
Identifiers: LCCN 2016042895 (print) | LCCN 2016048572 (ebook) | ISBN
   9781493026265 (hard cover) | ISBN 9781493026272 (e-book) | ISBN
   9781493026272 (ebook)
Subjects: LCSH: Gastronomy. | Food in popular culture. | Food writers.
Classification: LCC TX631 .N455 2017 (print) | LCC TX631 (ebook) | DDC
   641.01/3—dc23
LC record available at https://lccn.loc.gov/2016042895

Printed in the United States of America

Be smart, have fun, live life with flair.

—The Snob's maxim

CONTENTS

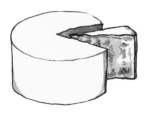

INTRODUCTION

This is a book for and about food snobs. But who, or what, is a food snob? It's a trickier and far more intriguing question than one might think at first.

For instance, Anthony Bourdain. He has described himself as "a born snob," and during his *Kitchen Confidential* days, when he was young and carousing his way around the restaurant kitchens of New York City, he said this about himself and a running buddy:

> We thought we were the only cooks in New York who could quote from the *Larousse Gastronomique*, *Repertoire de la Cuisine*, who knew who Vatel, Carême and Escoffier were, what Bocuse, Vergé and Guérard were doing across the water.

Such arcane knowledge (arcane outside the world of haute cuisine) might indeed be classified as snobby, but look at Bourdain's television programs. One of their hallmarks is his rollicking Hunter S. Thompson–like willingness to go down any dark alley or up any twisting mountain road to eat, drink, and explore new tastes—not qualities normally associated with snobs or snobbishness.

Alice Waters is another. She has been accused of being a snob—by Bourdain, among others. Her offense in their eyes is that she adheres too rigidly to a food ethic—local, fresh, sustainable, organic—that is out of touch with the real lives of ordinary people. It's elitist. Families and low-income people cannot afford to buy and eat organic all the time, unlike the well-off founder of Berkeley's Chez Panisse.

In defending herself, Waters has said that she would like nothing better than to extend the luxury of organic food to all, to make it more affordable, to help children and others, particularly in the

inner city, try their hand at gardening. Again, that's not exactly snobbish or elitist. Or is it?

Waters drew her early cooking inspiration (and still does) from France—the home of *haute cuisine, nouvelle cuisine, Repertoire de la Cuisine,* and Le Cordon Bleu, which trained Julia Child, the effervescent, quintessentially American cook who introduced millions to the art of French cooking. While Julia had strong likes and dislikes based on her training, intelligence, and sophistication, can anyone rightly call her snooty?

What about Roy Choi? He studied for a year at the Culinary Institute of America, Hyde Park, and apprenticed in the kitchen of Eric Ripert's Michelin three-star Le Bernardin, a "gastronomic temple" (to use an overworked food writer's phrase) of French food in New York City. But it would be a bit of a reach to classify the Korean-born, street-smart, tattooed, ex–low ridin' LA Kogi BBQ food truck guy as a snob, would it not?

Truth is, all of us have impulses and beliefs that are both snobbish and reverse snobbish, elitist and democratic, narrow and welcoming. All of us, that is, except perhaps for Lucy. When winter's first snowflakes started falling and her "Peanuts" pals stuck out their tongues to taste them, she sniffed, "I never eat December snowflakes. I always wait for January."

Here is how we view the matter in *Foodie Snob*. If you're a Lucy, if you have your own particular ideas on what's best, most exclusive, most daring, least known, avant-garde, tastiest, we respect that. We honor your opinion. Our goal is to support you in your quest to learn and taste and know as much as you can, while introducing you to new things or perhaps old things you weren't aware of.

This is not a book filled with "shoulds" and "musts." We would never presume to tell you what to think or eat, or how to do either. We see our role more as a presenter or curator, although yes, we too have strong opinions on certain matters and will offer them where it seems appropriate.

And what will you find on these pages? Holy *mole*! Flip back to the contents page and you'll get a much better sense than here. There are stories, lists, asides, advice, reviews, recommendations, discoveries, quotations, humor, snarky food fights galore, and interactive features like quizzes and match games. All the personalities mentioned so far in this tasting menu of an introduction are included in the book, plus Lidia Bastianich, Shakespeare, Auguste Gusteau, Gwyneth Paltrow, Ruth Reichl, Alice B. Toklas, Thomas Keller, Pete Wells, David Chang, Per Se, Il Vino, Giada De Laurentiis, Angelina Jolie and Brad Pitt, Lady and the Tramp, Matt Damon, Steve Jobs, John, Paul, George and Ringo, Simran Sethi, Michael Pollan, Nora Ephron, Cezanne, Luther Burbank, Homeboy Bakery, Tom Colicchio, and Adam and Eve.

And all those names you just read? *That's just the first chapter.*

True snobbery, as we see it, isn't just a matter of having an opinion; it has to do with knowing about the history and culture and language and romance of food—and oh yes, the people too, especially the people. The more you know about all these things, the more devastatingly brilliant your opinions will be.

Let's end the way we began: with AB. (But don't fret; he'll be back. He's like a Zelig character, popping up here and there in these pages and always stirring the pot.) Embroiled in, for God's sake, a controversy over cupcakes, one of the many controversies that chase him

around (and that he chases), Bourdain said, "It's not the cupcakes I have a problem with; it's cupcake mania. It's only a f**king cupcake."

This is, of course, pure nonsense. Bourdain knows better; he was probably just tweaking beaks. He and every other foodie knows in their heart of hearts that a cupcake is never just a cupcake, food is never just food. It is the whole f**king world. Let's have some fun.

—Kevin Nelson

CHAPTER ONE

A shared passion

THE COMMUNITY OF FOOD

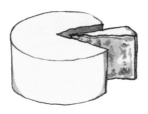

Everybody eats and most everybody cooks, and yet it is not eating or cooking per se that motivates those who love food. It is passion. Foodies are passionate about what they put in their mouths, and joyful when it turns out to be just the right thing. They feel a shared sense of community and history, and feel deeply about their likes and dislikes. In this chapter we talk about what brings food lovers together—and what splits them apart.

FOOD, A LOVE STORY

3 WORLD-CLASS CHEFS TELL WHY THEY LOVE FOOD AND COOKING

The Michelin three-star chef whose father left him as a boy. The Italian chef who vividly recalls her grandmother chopping *pestata* on a cutting board. The barbecue pitmaster who cooked his first pig and tasted moonshine for the first time on the same glorious day.

All food enthusiasts have stories to tell about how they came to love food; these stories, memories, and experiences partly form who they are. Here are three such stories, different but alike in their shared appreciation for the pleasures of coming together, at the table, with others.

THE SUPERSTAR CHEF

Thomas Keller did not grow up eating in restaurants like the French Laundry or Per Se, his two most acclaimed dining establishments. As a boy he ate Dinty Moore stew out of a can. "I've liked stew since I was a boy," he confides, "even when it was Dinty Moore out of a can, which it often was in a household of five kids and a working mother."

Born at Camp Pendleton near San Diego, Keller is the son of a Marine Corps drill instructor. But his father left the family when he was very young, and Betty, his auburn-haired mother, raised the boys on her

own, heading off to Florida to start their lives anew. There she found work as the manager of the Palm Beach Yacht Club, the starting point for her son's glittering culinary career. This was where he entered the restaurant business, starting as a pearl diver—old-school lingo for a dishwasher—before gradually moving up to cook.

"I wonder if I love the communal act of eating so much because throughout my childhood with four older brothers and a mom in the restaurant business, I spent a lot of time fending for myself, eating alone—and I recognized how eating together made all the difference," he recalls. "The best meals are the ones you eat with the people you care about."

In a bittersweet footnote to his story, later in life he reconciled with his father and got to do what he had missed out on as a boy: bonding with him over meals and drinks. Retired and in his eighties, Ed Keller moved to Yountville, California, where his famous son lived and had three of his restaurants, and the two became close. Ed became a well-known personality in town, greeting staff and customers at the French Laundry and having drinks in the garden across the street. On the last night of his life, his son made him barbecued chicken, his favorite, and shortcake with fresh strawberries enlivened by a shot of Grand Marnier. They sat and talked and had dinner together. He died the next day.

SNOB ADVICE

Yountville is a small, easily walkable restaurant town in Napa Valley. It's about an hour and a half north of San Francisco but well worth the drive. The French Laundry, Bouchon, and Ad Hoc are the three Keller restaurants there, and there are other fine places to eat in town and around the valley. As for Keller's Per Se in New York City, see what Pete Wells had to say about it on page 22.

THE ITALIAN CHEF

Lidia Bastianich's father loved to make *baccala mantecato*, a creamy dried cod dip or spread. "It was his culinary triumph," she says. "Every time I make it now, I remember him, with every bite."

This was in Pula, Istria, which was once part of Italy but is now Croatia, in the years after World War II when Lidia was an eager girl curious to learn, watching her grandmother make *pestata* by hand in their kitchen. "I can still hear the staccato clack-clack-clack of my grandmother's cleaver on a wooden board as she chopped the *pestata*." Her *nonna* would hand the cleaver to Lidia, who would dip it into a pot of boiling soup and then hand it back to her, and she'd go back to chopping. She says with a laugh that today she can make the garlic paste in ten minutes in a food processor.

At Christmastime in Istria her house was filled with the smells of the *baccala mantecato* her grandmother and parents were making, and when they went around to see other families during La Vigilia, the Feast of the Seven Fishes, that was what filled *their* homes too: the smell of dried codfish. These aromas were as much a part of Christmas Eve as Midnight Mass.

Escaping the Communist takeover of Yugoslavia in the 1950s, the Mattichio family—that is Bastianich's maiden name, and it appears in her byline for her books—reached America when she was twelve. Later she married Felice Bastianich, and they opened a restaurant in Queens. Since then, her little family business—in concert with Mario Batali and her children Joe Bastianich and Tanya Manuali—has grown into a national empire. But the little girl who watched her grandmother wield that cleaver with such skill hasn't changed fundamentally, even though she has become a doting grandmother herself.

"There should be no guilt in eating," she states firmly. "When we eat, we are nourishing our bodies, our minds, our souls. And we do it best with others, be it family, friends, or strangers."

THE PITMASTER

Ed Mitchell likes how cooking—and the eating that follows—helps people chill. "Any sort of grudges or arguments you have just sort of mellows out," he says. "It's just relaxing time."

Mitchell is a North Carolina barbecue pitmaster who made such an impression on Michael Pollan that Pollan featured him in his book *Cooked* and the Netflix series that followed it. Pollan, who lives in Berkeley, traveled to Mitchell's home in Wilson, about an hour from Raleigh in eastern North Carolina, had dinner with him and his mother, and studied him in action. Wearing a full white beard, baseball cap, and overalls, Mitchell specializes in what he calls "pit-cooked whole hog BBQ," a traditional Southern style that cooks the entire animal over a wood fire. Pollan dug the whole "primordial" vibe of it.

The James Beard Foundation and other city folks have celebrated Mitchell for being an authentic representative of American cooking traditions, and this is another thing he likes about what he does—how he occupies a place in a long line of pitmasters stretching back over

time. He tells the story about how, when he was a boy, he took over the pit and started barbecuing the pig when the pitmaster stepped away. When the old man came back and tasted what the boy had done, he rewarded Mitchell with his first slug of moonshine. "If you old enough to cook a pig like that," the old man told him, "you old enough to have moonshine." Mitchell recalls, "I was in heaven."

WILLIAM SHAKESPEARE: FOOD WRITER

Anthony Bourdain has described food writers as "a swamp. A petri dish of logrolling, cronyism, mendaciousness, greed, envy, collusion, corruption and willful self-deception." But surely he could not have been referring to one of the greatest food writers of all, William Shakespeare, who originated the phrase "eaten me out of house and home" and delivered many other tasty references in his plays. A brief sampling:

- "Asses, fools, dolts! Chaff and bran, chaff and bran! Porridge after meat!"—*Troilus and Cressida*
- "Why, then the world's mine oyster, which I with sword will open." —*The Merry Wives of Windsor*
- "My salad days, when I was green in judgment." —*Antony and Cleopatra*
- "Tis an ill cook that cannot lick his own fingers." —*Romeo and Juliet*
- "My lord of Ely, when I was last in Holborn I saw good strawberries in your garden there; I do beseech you send for some of them." —*Richard III*
- "With eager feeding, food doth choke the eater." —*ibid.*
- "I fear it is too choleric a meat. How say you to a fat tripe finely broiled?" —*The Taming of the Shrew*
- "If sack and sugar be a fault, God help the wicked! If to be old and merry be a sin, then many an old host that I know be damned." —*Henry IV, Part 1*

AND NOW, A WORD FROM CHEF GUSTEAU

A voice in haute cuisine that demands to be heard is that of Chef Auguste Gusteau, widely acclaimed as France's top chef, until a scathing review by a self-involved food critic knocked a star from his eponymous Paris restaurant and caused him to fall into a deep funk from which he never recovered.

His spirit lives on though, as evidenced by these excerpts from his international best seller, *Anyone Can Cook*:

- "You must not let anyone limit you because of where you come from. Your only limits are your soul. So it's true: Anyone can cook. But only the fearless can be great."
- "Good food is like music. It's color you can smell. And its excellence is all around you. You only need to be aware. To stop and savor it."
- "If you focus on what is behind, you will never be able to see ahead."
- "Food will come. Food always comes to those who love to cook."
- "Remy, you are a cook. A cook makes. A thief takes. You are not a thief." —*To his most famous protégée, Remy*
- "This much I knew. If you are what you eat, then I only want to eat the good stuff."—*Chef Remy, expressing words to live by*

FROM GWYNETH TO EVE

A HISTORY OF THE APPLE
IN 15 BACKWARD STEPS

In 2004 Gwyneth Paltrow and Chris Martin had their first child, a baby girl they named Apple. The name provoked widespread puzzlement and ridicule, although it is not clear why. A child named after a fruit? There are worse sins.

Indeed, one might argue that it is an inspired choice for a name, for the obvious reason that a fresh Fuji or Honeycrisp delivers such satisfyingly crunchy moments of pleasure. Nor is the apple just any fruit; it occupies a central place in American life and civilization as a whole. Can anyone doubt this? Moving backward in time from the birth of Apple Martin (No. 15), let us briefly review the long and glorious history of the apple.

14. In 2001 Ruth Reichl publishes *Comfort Me with Apples*, the second installment in her memoirs-with-recipes series. Whereas in the first book she recalls her childhood years and her mother's awful, life-endangering cooking—"My mission," she writes, "was to keep Mom from killing anybody at dinner"—the sequel charts her romantic

ups-and-downs as she begins her climb up the publishing food chain (*New West*, *Los Angeles Times*, *New York Times*, *Gourmet*). The title alludes to a verse in "The Song of Solomon" in which a young love-torn woman sings, "Stay me with flagons, comfort me with apples: for I am sick of love." Years later a food critic would write a spoof of her book called *Comfort Me with Offal*.

13. The year 1999 sees the invention of the apple martini or "apple-tini," a vodka martini with a wedge of apple, apple liqueurs, or apple juice (there are many variations). Although people have drunk gin or vodka with apple juice for eons, the appletini raises the apple's profile in the hot new category of artisan cocktails. "What cocktail could be more Big Apple?" asks New York food writer Rick Marin. "One a day keeps the therapist away! Too bad it was invented in Los Angeles." It was also Zach Braff's favorite drink, used for comic effect on *Scrubs*.

12. In a scene from 1997's *Good Will Hunting*, Matt Damon, playing a gifted but troubled mathematician from the wrong side of the tracks, meets Minnie Driver at a Cambridge bar. Like every Cambridge bar from the time of John Adams on, it is packed with obnoxious, self-absorbed university students, one of whom is trying to hit on Minnie. But Matt is the one who scores and gets her phone number, after which he walks over to his rival seated on a stool at the bar.

"You like apples?" Damon asks him.

The guy is puzzled by the question, but says yeah, he likes apples.

Damon holds up the paper with Driver's phone number on it and says, "How do you like them apples?" Then walks out in triumph.

Footnote: In real life, Damon's mother was a schoolteacher, and she surely received apples as gifts from appreciative students.

11. In the late 1970s two clever young guys named Steve decide to start a computer company in Menlo Park, California, but they're not sure what to call it. One of the Steves, last name Jobs, who is a fad dieter and currently on a fruitarian diet, has just returned from a stay at an apple farm where his chores included pruning Gravenstein trees. Talking it over with the other Steve, last name Wozniak, he thinks they should call their new company Apple because it sounds "fun, spirited, and not intimidating." Wozniak, who is himself a fun and spirited guy, agrees.

The two Steves are of course aware of the legendary role of the apple in the advancement of science and human progress—falling on Isaac Newton's head that day, whilst he was sitting under a tree in his garden. One of Apple's greatest successes was the Macintosh and one of its greatest failures the Newton.

10. James Beard publishes, in 1972, his definitive work on American cookery containing twenty-two pages of recipes that reference apples and applesauce. Even before America was a country, generations upon generations ate applesauce for dessert and as a side for pork chops. As for apple pie, it is, well, as American as apple pie. "So common has apple pie always been in this country—although it did not originate here—that many old American cookbooks did not bother to give a recipe," writes Beard. "It was taken for granted that every housewife had her own favorite." Those were the days, he adds in a sweetly nostalgic tone, "when people had apple trees in their backyards."

9. In 1968 four Liverpool blokes named John, Paul, George, and Ringo form a record company, which they call Apple Corps. The name—it's Paul's idea—stems from the Magritte painting, "The Son of Man," of a man in a suit and bowler hat, his face obscured by a green apple. Although things work out pretty well for the four fellows, their record

label achieves only limited success, later suing Apple Computer for illegally infringing on its name and trademark. The two Apples engage in a long legal battle that is finally resolved a few years after the birth of Apple Martin. Fortunately, attorneys for the two companies do not sue her parents for infringing on the Apple name.

8. The decade of the 1950s was the last great era of transcontinental train travel, and the Northern Pacific Railway—it ran across the northern states between Lake Superior and Seattle—was renowned for the quality of its dining service and meals, in particular a baked apple "monumental in size and wonderful to eat," in the words of James Beard who had the pleasure of doing so.

Both the baked apple and a giant baked potato, also pleasing to Beard's palate, were regionally sourced, although no one in those days would have ever used such a phrase. The potatoes were grown in Idaho and the apples in Washington, which remains a big apple-growing state today. One more famous Northern Pacific dish: Washington apple pan cake.

7. According to etymologist Barry Popik, it is a date certain: January 15, 1920. That was the day the phrase "The Big Apple" came into being. On a trip to the South to watch the ponies run, New York horse-racing writer John J. Fitz Gerald overheard some stable

hands at a New Orleans track mention "the big apple," which was a new term to him. The men were referring to what's common knowledge on a farm but what people in the city tend to forget: Horses love to eat apples.

Fitz Gerald started dropping The Big Apple into his sports columns for the *New York Morning Telegraph,* but it didn't move outside the realm of horse racing until Walter Winchell and Hollywood screenwriters picked up on it as a catch phrase for New York City itself. "I'm sending yuh a couple of trailers, with tin shirts—gorillas from th' Big Apple," writes one Runyonesque scribe mimicking Chicago mobster slang of this era. "We shoot tonight—or somebody gets taken for a ride."

6. "I want to astonish Paris with an apple," says Paul Cezanne, and so he does, in 1898, with the opening of his exhibition of Impressionist paintings entitled "Still Life with Apples." This exhibit becomes the talk of Paris because of its focus on the lowly apple—a fruit so ordinary that horses eat it. Cezanne's genius also forces the gallery-going public to reconsider its views on the still life, previously regarded as the artistic equivalent of an apple and not a fit subject for serious painters. Cezanne's treatment of apples, bread, eggs, lemons, and other ordinary food items inspires future artists to find meaning and high art in the commonplace, such as Andy Warhol and his "Campbell's Soup Cans."

5. Influenced by Charles Darwin and his views on natural selection, Luther Burbank, a thirty-six-year-old Massachusetts-born horticulturist, moves to California, in 1885, and establishes a farm on Gold Ridge in Sebastopol, near Santa Rosa. This fertile fifteen-acre plot of land, its climate ideal for gardening, he dubs his "Experiment Farm."

His experiments consist of crossing foreign and native strains of plants to create new seedlings, which he grafts onto plants. He con-

ducts thousands of experiments at a time involving millions of plants, and his work pushes the science of growing things into a new age. Over his career he develops hundreds of new varieties of fruits, nuts, flowers, and vegetables—among them Santa Rosa plums, Freestone peaches, and those Idaho potatoes so beloved by Northern Pacific passengers. At Experiment Farm, which can be visited today, one apple tree planted by Burbank contains twenty-five grafts. "That's twenty-five different kinds of apples," a preservation society member notes. "They blossom and ripen at different times."

4. In 1845, the most celebrated figure in the history of apples dies. His name was John Chapman, better known as Johnny Appleseed, who actually did carry a bag of apple seeds around with him as he walked the countryside, planting trees and preaching the virtues of apples to settlers in Pennsylvania, Ohio, and Indiana during America's westward expansion.

But in Johnny Appleseed's time, apples were not the eating fruit they are today; they were too sour for that—"sour enough," as Thoreau wrote, "to set a squirrel's teeth on edge and make a jay scream." They were called *spitters* and mashed up into hard cider, a popular alcoholic drink that was outlawed during Prohibition. Suddenly faced with a ban on hard cider, apple growers shifted their marketing message to promote the nutritional and health benefits of their products. Thus, the adage was born: An apple a day keeps the doctor away.

3. John Milton writes the greatest epic poem of the English language, *Paradise Lost*, which, for all its many virtues, is a hit piece on the apple. In it he fingers the fruit for assisting in the ruin of Adam and Eve and by implication, all of humanity in that sorry business in the Garden of Eden. "The fruit of that forbidden tree, whose mortal taste brought death into the world, and all our woe," he writes in his 1667 masterwork.

Impossible as it is to believe today, poets of Milton's stature were among society's most powerful and influential figures, feared and respected by kings. And so it mattered when he went beyond the generic description of "forbidden fruit" and called the culprit out by name: "Him by fraud I have seduc'd from his Creator," he writes in the guise of Eve, "with an Apple."

2. The first English settlers arrive in Jamestown, in 1607, beginning an overseas migration in which waves of English and European settlers will come to the new world in search of a new life—a new life, yes, but with an old familiar friend. While apple trees are said to originate from present-day Kazakhstan, it was the ancient Romans who refined grafting, taking the stem of one apple tree and inserting it into the stock of another. Early American settlers, being farmers who worked the land, understood these techniques and brought apple stems and buds with them across the waters.

Granted the trees that grew from these stems produced bitter-tasting spitters, but this was where those inventive Colonial cooks and home bakers worked their magic, creating apple butter, apple snow, applesauce cookies, apple fruit leather, fried apple rings, caramel apple rings, sweet potato and apple pie—a Southern variation—apple pan dowdy, apple dumplings, and apple brown Betty. Pie back then was spelled with a *y*; settlers ate meat pyes, game pyes, and apple pyes for breakfast.

1. In Genesis, the apple is never named. The fruit hanging from the Tree of the Knowledge of Good and Evil, the fruit the serpent tempts Eve with, and the fruit that Eve and Adam eat—it is nothing more than that: *fruit*. Early translators turned the fruit into an apple, and over the centuries church scholars and writers like Milton have pushed this idea onto an unsuspecting public and transformed it into a common, albeit false, belief. Which leads one to ask: If the apple story in the

Book of Genesis is nothing more than a tall tale, like Johnny Apple-seed or Newton and his apple tree, could other Biblical stories be tall tales as well?

Oh Lordy, heaven help us. Sit down, have a piece of fresh-baked pie still warm from the oven. Put a scoop of vanilla ice cream on it. You'll feel better after you eat something.

THEY BIT THE APPLE

4 CELEBRITY COUPLES
AND THE ROMANCE OF FOOD

Food provides comfort and solace after a breakup, and couples share meals in those early days when love and hope are blooming. The best moments and memories of every relationship often center on meals.

It is a complicated relationship—food and romance. Here are four celebrity couples, sketches of their dining experiences together, and the Snob's dating advice on how we may learn from them.

ANGELINA JOLIE AND BRAD PITT
When in Paris, when things were going swimmingly for them, one of their favorite spots was Il Vino near the Place des Invalides in the 7th arrondissement. It has a unique approach, and you can see why

the world's formerly most glamorous celebrity couple might enjoy it. At Il Vino people first choose the wine they would like to drink; then, based on that, the chef prepares a dinner that will best pair with their wine choices. The owner is Enrico Bernardo, among the world's best sommeliers, and there are fifteen hundred items on the Il Vino wine list. Brad took Angelina there to celebrate her birthday after the French opening of *World War Z*; it was reported they had langoustines, cake, and "French wine," which hardly tells us anything.

Down in the south of France, for the Cannes Film Festival, Brangelina dined at Tetou in the tiny Cote d'Azur hideaway of Golfe Juan between Cannes and Antibes. They liked Tetou because it's private—they sat in the back, away from any windows where they might be photographed by the paparazzi—and it has a charming old-timey French look and feel. Hollywood royalty and the rich have been going there since the 1920s; there's a private beach across the street. The founder, Ernest Cirio, was the self-styled "Le Roi du Bouillabaisse," and this was what they ordered: bouillabaisse, a tart, and wine. The media breathlessly reported that Pitt paid cash for the meal, which is required at Tetou. It accepts cash only, no credit cards.

One last Brangelina meal, this one back home in the United States before their split. TMZ broke the news that Brad and Angelina, with their small army of children in tow, stopped in at a Subway in Glendale one afternoon and ordered "two Meatball Marinara footlongs, one chicken teriyaki sandwich, and a few kids' meals." They paid forty-four dollars cash, left a six-dollar tip, and took the order to go.

Snob's dating advice: Until things went awry for them, Pitt was clearly doing some things right. For his wife's birthday he treated her to a nice meal at a pricey restaurant—a good strategy early in a relationship when you're trying to impress your date. Jolie was clearly doing some things right as well; for the Tetou dinner and after-party,

she glided through the evening in a striking custom black Yves Saint Laurent suit. It is difficult, however, to draw too many conclusions based on such limited information. Angelina doesn't eat much, we can see that. If only we knew who had the meatball sub and who had the chicken.

NORA EPHRON AND CARL BERNSTEIN

The late Nora Ephron, a writer, screenwriter, and director of luminous wit and talent, had three husbands. Whenever she fell in love, she expressed her feelings through her cooking. "I have friends who begin with pasta, and friends who begin with rice," she wrote, "but whenever I fall in love, I begin with potatoes." Two of her lovestruck potato dishes were hash browns–style Swiss potatoes and potatoes Anna.

Her second husband was Carl Bernstein, the ex-*Washington Post* journalist who shall forever be remembered as the man who was "capable of having sex with a Venetian blind," in Ephron's immortal line, as well as other minor investigative reportorial achievements in his career. Ephron delivered this zinger in *Heartburn*, her autobiographical novel with recipes—you can find the two potato dishes in there. It chronicles her bitter breakup with Bernstein, who had an affair when she was pregnant with their child. Ephron describes her rounded belly during this period as looking like "a Casaba melon," and in her bad moments she liked to take shots at her husband's lover, mainly for her lousy cooking. "A carrot cake that I'd made had too much crushed pineapple in it but was still awfully good compared to Thelma's desserts," she sniped. "Thelma always makes these gluey puddings."

Snob's dating advice: Potato dishes *are* good for romance—and entertaining. Hannah Plumb and James Russell, the British husband and wife designers, like potato dauphinoise because they can make

it together, slicing and peeling while catching up on the other's news. A truly wonderful dish to make for your lover is risotto. Judith Barrett and Norma Wasserman's *Risotto* is a classic. And men, stay away from the Venetian blinds.

SNOB ASIDE

One of Ephron's literary heroes was Lillian Hellman, and Hellman's pot roast recipe is in *Heartburn*. Known for her caustic intelligence and plays such as *The Little Foxes*, Hellman grew up in New York and New Orleans and was, by all accounts, a wonderful cook, particularly adept at the Southern dishes she learned as a girl. Her cookbook, *Eating Together*, contained recipes for crayfish and turtle soup, but she never lived to see it in print, dying just before its publication in 1984.

MARIA SHRIVER AND ARNOLD SCHWARZENEGGER

To be honest, we know next to nothing about Arnold and Maria's love life and their now-terminated marriage except for the standard gossip (Arnold, you idiot!), and frankly that is how we prefer to keep it. But we mention them because it gives us the chance to tell an old Jay Leno joke about Arnold and Maria that has to do with food, couples, and dating, and even has a movie reference in it.

How did Arnold ask Maria out on their first date?

"Eat Drink Man Woman."

Snob's dating advice: Humor is always good, including silliness from time to time. Women like it, men like it, and tactfully employed it can get you through those awkward and tense moments early in a relationship. Perhaps you or your date is having butternut squash soup or a roasted butternut squash on the side. This may be the perfect moment to recall the Jimmy Fallon line from one of his Thank You Notes bits, where he gives thanks to ordinary things such as but-

ternut squash. "Thank you butternut squash for being an appetizing food . . . despite having butt, nut, and squash in your name."

LADY AND THE TRAMP

A more perfect couple and setting could not be imagined than the Lady and the Tramp at Tony's Town Square Restaurant, established in 1912. Lady, sweet and beautifully coiffed, whose name was Darling, and the Tramp, scruffy and street-savvy, had the place to themselves. It was quiet, private, and intimate.

"Now tell me, what's your pleasure," asked Tony, the gregarious and mustachioed owner and head waiter. "A la carte? Dinner?"

The Tramp barked an answer that Tony understood immediately, relaying it to his cook: "He wants the two spaghetti e-special, heavy on zuh meat-uh-ball." Not sure how Tony knew that, the cook nonetheless produced a gorgeous plate of spaghetti that Tony pronounced "the best spaghetti in town" when he set it in front of the shy young couple.

As Darling and her date began to eat, Tony and the cook, on accordion and guitar respectively, serenaded them with a song, *"Bella Notte,"* with Tony absolutely slaying the vocals: "Oh this is the night, when the heavens are right, on this lovely bella notte . . ."

As the third verse began, Lady delicately picked up a single strand of spaghetti and started to suck it into her mouth. Tramp was looking away, but then he went to eat too and suddenly the two of them were on opposite ends of the same strand without knowing it. They kept eating and sucking on the pasta strand until their lips met in a kiss. Lady turned away in embarrassment, and the dashing Tramp responded by pushing a meatball over to her on the plate, Lady's eyes lighting up with love.

Snob's dating advice: Spaghetti is not a classic first-date dish because it can get messy. Still, it's hard to go wrong with the Italians in anything having to do with food or romance. They know what they're doing. Addendum: George Givot voiced Tony and sang *"Bella Notte,"* and Peggy Lee, the voice of Darling, wrote the lyrics.

ALICE B. TOKLAS AND HER COOKBOOK

Nora Ephron and Ruth Reichl both wrote books in a literary genre that may be described as "memoirs with recipes." One of the earliest and most charming memoirs of this type is the *Alice B. Toklas Cook Book*—cookbook was two words back then—written by Alice herself.

In it she recounts her culinary life and adventures in France and the United States with her partner Gertrude Stein. These were the 1920s and '30s, when visitors such as Mr. and Mrs. Ernest Hemingway would come to visit them in their Paris flat. Alice would retreat into the kitchen with the women, while Gertrude, a writer and intellectual, would sit in the front room with the men smoking cigars and drinking.

How lucky we are that Alice spent so much time in the kitchen! (No doubt Gertrude and her guests felt the same.) The book contains recipes given to her by chefs at restaurants in Paris and around the French countryside and the dishes she made for their bookish and artsy friends. Once she prepared a striped bass poached in dry white wine for Picasso. Before serving the dish she covered the fish in ordinary mayonnaise, and with a pastry tube she decorated it with red mayonnaise and tomato paste. She then added sieved hard-boiled eggs—the whites and yolks apart—truffles, and herbs.

"I was proud of my chef d'oeuvre when it was served and Picasso exclaimed at its beauty," she wrote. Not many cooks can claim a compliment like that.

Over the years Alice has become associated with fudge brownies laced with hashish, but this was not her recipe. No such recipe appeared in the first American edition of the book published by Harper & Brothers in 1954. Her British publishers put it in their edition—it was added by a friend of Alice's, with her approval—and it drew such attention that it has appeared in all subsequent editions of this highly recommended classic.

MATCH GAME 1

PETE WELLS SLAMS
THOMAS KELLER'S PER SE

It was the review heard 'round the world. On January 22, 2016, Pete Wells, restaurant reviewer for the *New York Times*, published a devastating critique of Per Se, the Michelin three-star New York restaurant of Thomas Keller, one of America's most revered chefs—"Saint Thomas," Anthony Bourdain has called him.

Here is a wickedly fascinating match game from Wells's 7.0 Richter scale review (the aftershocks of which continue to be felt in the restaurant world). In the left column are comments from the review; on the right is the Per Se item Wells was referring to. But not everything he said was critical; a couple positives are in the mix too. Your job is to match the dis with the dish. Find the answers on page 35 after the Julia quiz.

What Wells said . . .	Keller's Per Se
"A swampy mess"	The service
"murky and appealing as bong water"	fried eggplant raviolo
"fat envelopes of pure pleasure"	Per Se itself
"American playfulness, rigorous finesse"	lobster
"the oblivious sleepwalking"	mushroom pot pie
"limp, dispiriting"	Keller's cooking style
"tasted like peanut butter to which something terrible had been done"	salmon tartare, oysters in pearls
"intransigently chewy: gristle of the sea"	risotto
"a few pieces of heirloom furniture"	chestnut puree
"hermetic, self-regarding, ungenerous"	agnolotti with squash
"it felt like extortion"	matsutake mushroom bouillon
"Familiar but transporting"	yam dumplings

MORE SHARPENING OF THE KNIVES

WELLS REDUX, AND VAUCLUSE STRIKES BACK

For all the changes in the world of food in the past two decades, one fundamental truth still applies: *The New York Times* remains the most powerful single voice in restaurant criticism, especially in New York. What its reviewer says, matters.

It mattered a great deal when Pete Wells sliced and diced Per Se, and it matters when he flashes his rhetorical knives at other eateries in Manhattan and elsewhere. Here is a choice sampling.

GIADA, THE LAS VEGAS RESTAURANT OF GIADA DE LAURENTIIS

"There is little doubt whose place it is. Ms. De Laurentiis is invoked so often that it can seem she wants you to feel as if you're in her museum. The board of flatbread and grissini says it's 'Giada's bread selection,' and the plate of thumbprint and 'mega-chip' cookies is 'Giada's cookie selection.' Her words, familiar to her television audience, are even repeated in six chandeliers around the dining room, cut out in silhouette so that light beams from behind: 'I eat a little bit of Everything and not a lot of Anything.'

"As a quotation for posterity, this is not exactly 'Et tu, Brute.' But it may describe Ms. De Laurentiis's philosophy for food at Giada. All of it is in a relaxed, approachable California-Italian mode, and none of it is very hard to leave on the plate."

GUY'S AMERICAN KITCHEN & BAR, GUY FIERI'S NEW YORK CITY RESTAURANT

"Guy Fieri, have you eaten at your new restaurant in Times Square? Have you pulled up one of the 500 seats at Guy's American Kitchen & Bar and ordered a meal? Did you eat the food?

"What exactly about a small salad with four or five miniature croutons makes Guy's Famous Big Bite Caesar a) big b) famous or c) Guy's, in any meaningful sense?

"Were you struck by how very far from awesome the Awesome Pretzel Chicken Tenders are?

"Hey, did you try that blue drink, the one that glows like nuclear waste? Any idea why it tastes like some combination of radiator fluid and formaldehyde?

"What accounts for the vast difference between the Donkey Sauce recipe you've published and the Donkey Sauce in your restaurant? And when we hear the words Donkey Sauce, which part of the donkey are we supposed to think about?"

KAPPO MASA, A JAPANESE RESTAURANT ON MADISON AVENUE (CO-OWNED BY MASAYOSHI TAKAYAMA OF MASA)

"If you are one of those people who suspects that Manhattan is being remade as a private playground for millionaires who either don't mind spending hundreds of dollars for mediocrity or simply can't tell the difference, Kappo Masa is not going to convince you that you're wrong.

"Kappo Masa provides a pantomime of service without the substance, and the restaurant itself is an imitation of luxury, not the real thing."

MOMOFUKU NISHI, A DAVID CHANG RESTAURANT IN CHELSEA

"Too much of the cooking at Nishi is self-reverential, inward looking and so concerned with technique. In his early days, Mr. Chang served the kind of food chefs like to eat: intense, animalistic, O.K. with messiness, indifferent to prettiness. Nishi serves the kind of food chefs cook to impress one another."

LE TURTLE, A FRENCH PLACE ON THE LOWER EAST SIDE

"The chef, Greg Proechel . . . seems to have no idea how to translate the French new wave into edible form. Intelligently, he stays away from Godard references; there is no A Bout de Souffle au Chocolat. But he also stays away from anything you could really call French cooking.

"And while Mr. Proechel gets some deep flavors out of his braised oxtail, he's had the meat trimmed into long sections that are interwoven with equally long sections of connective tissue: after awhile, it starts to feel more like dissection than eating."

VAUCLUSE, A FRENCH RESTAURANT HEADED BY CHEF MICHAEL WHITE

"Much of the menu lassos the grayest of old gray mares and drags them out for one last trot around the paddock. Some of the mares are revived by exercise. Others, like the chocolate mousse that has been repeatedly violated by bits of baked cocoa meringue and buried under chocolate ice cream, seem as if they would rather be left alone to live out their retirements in peace.

"The potato tart is a jumble of sliced fingerlings, lardons, bits of Camembert and truffles waiting for something to happen. Nothing is going to happen as long as they're all loafing on a crackerlike crust that you could safely serve to a patient on a no-flavor diet.

"So many of the recipes seem to contain the instruction 'Fold the butter into the butter.' A dizzying slick of it clung to the egg noodles."

It must be noted that in all these reviews Wells mixed flattering comments in with the less than flattering. This hardly satisfied the CEO of Vaucluse's ownership group, Ahmass Fakahany, who delivered a blistering critique of Wells in an open letter to him published on the company's website. "I am writing you because over the course of time you need to know you are losing credibility," Fakahany wrote. "The New York Times Dining review section is at its lowest point, and the subject of much industry chatter in this regard. Congratulations. You have managed to do a fantastic job of getting it there."

He continued, "You need to do some of the basic journalism and sharpen your food knowledge, please—and actually show you love it as we do. You cut corners in your haste to develop preconceived notions and to get quickly to silly childish jabs. Your fact checking questions reveal consistently an embarrassing lack of knowledge." He went on. "You seem so desperately anxious to be relevant in your time in this post. Is it because you want to develop a personal profile knowing you will never be a Craig Claiborne, Mimi Sheraton, Ruth Reichl, Frank Bruni or a Florence Fabricant?"

Leaving aside the monumental question of where Wells fits into the pantheon of food and dining writers for the *Times*, there does seem to be an awful lot of—well, we do not normally like to use this word, but it seems awfully apt in this case—*bitchiness* in the food world, no? More instances of it will follow in this book, to be sure.

As for Thomas Keller, he decided, perhaps wisely, to observe the axiom about not picking fights with those who buy their ink by the truckload. After the Wells review he maintained a dignified silence for a time before issuing an apology. "The fact that the New York Times restaurant critic Pete Wells's dining experiences did not live up to his expectations and to ours is greatly disappointing to me and to my team," he wrote. "We are sorry we let you down."

THE SNOB 8

EAT. DO GOOD. EAT SOME MORE

"It has long been apparent," wrote Craig Claiborne, "that people who dote on cooking are among the most generous people on earth."

They are generous for the same reason they sometimes take out the knives and wield them against one another: They care deeply about food and its life-giving qualities. Amid the countless food banks, soup kitchens, shelters, faith ministries, holiday giving, meals on wheels, civic spaghetti and crab feeds, charity food endeavors, and food businesses that donate to worthy causes, here are eight projects that in different ways seek to bring the pleasures and blessings of good food to the wider population.

HOMEBOY BAKERY

Homeboy Bakery of Los Angeles sells bread, scones, bagels, and pastries that are baked on the premises by young men who are trained in the techniques of making cake, pastry, laminated dough, bread, and rolls.

So what, right? Everybody does that. But these young bakers-in-training are not the usual: They're former gangbangers who have done time in prison and are attempting to put their lives back together by working real jobs and receiving real job training at Homeboy Industries, a nonprofit corporation that oversees the bakery, a diner, the Homegirl Café (which is staffed by ex-convict females), and food stands at farmers' markets around Los Angeles.

Homeboy Bakery began in 1992 after the Los Angeles riots when Father Greg Boyle, the pastor of the Dolores Mission in the Boyles Heights neighborhood, recognized the need to help inner-city Latino and black males find an alternative to gangs and violence. Every month more than a thousand ex-gang members walk through the doors of the bakery looking for a chance to start a new life. HomeboyIndustries.org

BROAD STREET MINISTRY

Philadelphia's Broad Street Ministry feeds more than a thousand homeless and hungry people every week. But Bill Golderer emphasizes that what they do there is not a soup kitchen or shelter.

Rather, what the Broad Street Hospitality Collaborative does is provide its "guests"—this is the word Golderer, a minister, uses—a dining experience that treats them with "dignity and delight." The meals are prepared by an executive chef and are not served cafeteria style. The guests sit at tables where the volunteer waitstaff takes their orders

and serves them like in a restaurant. They eat on tables with table-cloths in the upstairs dining room of the church.

Golderer calls this concept "radical hospitality," and a big reason why it works is the support of Philadelphia's restaurant community. Philly restaurateurs Steven Cook and Mike Solomonov donate all of the net profits of their Rooster Soup Co. diner to Broad Street. Tria, Sweet Box, Rittenhouse Hotel, and other restaurants also participate in fundraising programs for it. BroadStreetHospitality.org

FEEDING AMERICA

Feeding America, formerly known as Second Harvest, is a nation-wide network of food banks. It originated when a retired business-man named John van Hengel began volunteering at a soup kitchen in Phoenix in the late 1960s. The kitchen kept running out of food, and one day van Hengel saw a mother scouring a grocery store trash bin hoping to find something to feed her family. He talked to her, and she told him how she wished food banks were like money banks—places where food could be deposited for later use.

This gave van Hengel an idea and he acted upon it, establishing the country's first food bank, the St. Mary's Food Bank. The Phoenix com-munity rallied behind the concept; individuals, families, Cub Scouts, Boy Scouts, for-profit companies, nonprofit civic groups such as the Rotary and Lions clubs, and many others collected and contributed cans of food, or donated and raised money that was used to pur-chase food. That first year St. Mary's distributed 275,000 pounds of food to people in need.

Gradually more cities followed Phoenix's lead and founded food banks of their own, with van Hengel organizing them into a national concern. Feeding America provides meals and food for tens of mil-lions of people every year. FeedingAmerica.org

THE EDIBLE SCHOOLYARD

Every day on her way to Chez Panisse, Alice Waters would drive past Martin Luther King Jr. Middle School in Berkeley, thinking how neglected and uncared for the school looked. She commented about this in the local paper, and the school principal, Neil Smith, saw the article and called her to come by and visit Martin Luther King to see if there was some way the two of them could join forces to make things better for the students.

Thus was born the Edible Schoolyard Project, now a national program whose goal is to give students hands-on lessons in the value of good food, nutrition, and gardening. The pilot school for the project is Martin Luther King, and it remains a model of what Waters and her associates would like to establish at schools around the nation. It features a garden (originally it was a one-acre slab of asphalt that was torn up and planted with a cover crop) and a kitchen; children grow food, cook what they've grown, and then share it together at the table. EdibleSchoolyard.org

THE CHILE PEPPER INSTITUTE

Born in Mexico and brought to this country as a baby by his grandmother, Fabian Garcia became a member of New Mexico State University's first graduating class, in 1894. After a year of graduate work at Cornell, he returned home to teach horticulture and begin work on what would become the quest of his lifetime, the development of the New Mexico chile pepper.

Farmers grew chile peppers in those days, but could never count on them as a reliable crop. No one knew how large or small the pods would be or even what varieties of peppers were in the ground. Nor could consumers be sure of what they were getting. Too hot? Not hot enough? Enter Garcia, who, after years of trial and error, devel-

oped what is known as "New Mexico No. 9," the first standardized New Mexico chile pepper.

Garcia was to the chile pepper what Luther Burbank was to the Santa Rosa plum or Freestone peach. His innovations led to the creation of the chile pepper industry and the arrival of red and green peppers, hot and mild, on store shelves. The international Chile Pepper Institute, located on the New Mexico State campus in Las Cruces, continues his work as a nonprofit research and education center devoted to the *Capsicum*, or chile pepper. ChilePepperInstitute.org

GO EAT GIVE
Sucheta Rawal is a Georgia native of Indian descent whose company, Go Eat Give, combines food and travel with art, music, and dancing to promote cultural understanding. It sponsors trips within the United States as well as to Cuba, Kenya, Indonesia, and India. Travelers take cooking classes and eat in the homes of locals while volunteering in the areas where they're staying.

Go Eat Give also sponsors what it calls "destination dinners" in Atlanta and Washington DC. It invites people of different races and backgrounds to break bread together at various local ethnic restaurants. They meet and talk, hear speakers, and, it is hoped, chip away at the barriers that keep them apart. GoEatGive.com

MUSEUM OF FOOD AND DRINK
This young but ambitious Brooklyn museum-in-the-making seeks to inform people about the history, culture, and science of gastronomy. It currently holds cooking workshops and demos in the restaurant-rich Brooklyn neighborhood of Williamsburg, and many of New York's hot stove glitterati—Mario Batali, David Chang, Wylie Dufresne, Elizabeth Falkner, Alex Guarnaschelli— serve on its advisory boards. Mofad.org

FOOD POLICY ACTION

Tom Colicchio is best known as a judge on Top Chef and the chef and owner of Craft and other restaurants. But as the cofounder of Food Policy Action, a Washington DC food advocacy group, he has a fiery political side too. "As soon as one legislator loses their job over the way they vote on hunger issues and food issues," he says, "we're going to send a clear message to Congress that we're organized, we're viable, we're strong, and yes, we have a food movement." One of the group's most urgent priorities is clearer food labeling, particularly for genetically modified foods, and it publishes a scorecard that rates senators and representatives on how they measure up on food issues. FoodPolicyAction.org

FOODIE SNOB QUIZ #1

HOW WELL DO YOU KNOW JULIA?

An American in Paris, a woman succeeding in a man's world, author of a paradigm-shifting cookbook, the ebullient and eccentric star of a hit television cooking program that also shifted paradigms, and a woman in love—in so many ways Julia Child embodied the food and cooking branch of the Great American Dream. But how well do you know her and her legacy? Take this quiz and find out. Answers follow the quiz.

1. "For me the truth always lies with Julia," said a respected chef not commonly associated with French cuisine. "How can you

doubt the one who taught you to master hollandaise and puff pastry?" Who said this?

   a. Roy Choi

   b. Susan Feniger

   c. Rick Bayless

   d. David Chang

2. Another quote from a well-known female chef and food personality: "When I was first married, I studied Julia Child's *Mastering the Art of French Cooking* as if it were the Bible." Name her. (Hint—and this will be a dead giveaway to her fans: Her husband is Jeffrey.)

   a. Martha Stewart

   b. Patricia Wells

   c. Ina Garten

   d. Lidia Bastianich

3. When Julia graduated from Smith College in 1930 with a degree in history, she never dreamed of becoming a famous cook and personality. To what occupation did she aspire?

   a. novelist

   b. teacher

   c. doctor

   d. librarian

4. It is well-known that during World War II Julia worked for the OSS, a forerunner to the CIA. Less well-known is the fact that before joining the OSS Julia applied to join the two women's branches of the armed services, the WACS and WAVES. Both turned her down, though. Why?

   a. She could not cook, a condition of employment for servicewomen at the time.

   b. She was not mechanical, also what the services were looking for.

   c. She had poor eyesight.

   d. At six foot two, she was too tall.

5. So esteemed is Julia's reputation that many people do not realize she was not the sole author of *Mastering the Art of French Cooking*. Even some foodies can't name her two coauthors. Can you?

a. Simone Beck and Aimee Cassiot

b. Simone Beck and Louisette Bertholle

c. Simone Beck and Avis De Voto

d. Simone de Beauvoir and Jean-Paul Sartre

6. Here's an easy one. Or is it? Every Julia devotee can tell you that she trained at Le Cordon Bleu, the Parisian cooking school. But not every devotee knows what the school's name means in English. Translate, please.

a. The Blue Watch

b. The Blue Rope or String

c. The Blue Line

d. The Blue Ribbon

7. In Nora Ephron's film *Julie & Julia*, Knopf book editor Judith Jones cooks a recipe from *Mastering the Art of French Cooking*, which was as yet unpublished. The dish she cooks—leading her to greenlight the book and publish it—is the same one Julia prepared on the first program of The French Chef in 1963. What was it?

a. boeuf bourguignon

b. cheese soufflé

c. roast duck a l'orange

d. grilled whole chicken

8. *Julie & Julia* tells two interlocking stories—Julia's adventures in France in the 1950s and those of contemporary food writer Julia Powell, who cooked every recipe in *Mastering the Art of French Cooking* and blogged about it. The last meal Powell, played by Amy Adams, prepares in the film is one she had been dreading for a year. What did she need to do that so disturbed her?

a. clean and de-ink squid

b. soak and peel a calf's brain

c. bone a duck

d. skewer the rump knucklebone of a lamb

9. Julia Child wrote, "He was a great inspiration, his enthusiasm about wine and food helped to shape my tastes and his encouragement saw me through discouraging moments." To whom was she referring?

a. Chef Max Bugnard, her mentor at Le Cordon Bleu

b. Paul Child, her husband

c. Russell Morash, producer and director of *The French Chef*

d. Dan Ackroyd, who did a famous spoof of her on *Saturday Night Live*. Julia saw the show, enjoyed it, and released this tongue-in-cheek statement about it.

10. In 2016 Twitch, an online video-game streaming service, showed back-to-back-to-back episodes of The French Chef for four consecutive days. This marathon showing attracted more than a million viewers—mostly teenage boy gamers—and spurred Twitch to stream another old-time Julia cooking show. What was the title of this award-winning PBS show that introduced her good friend Jacques Pepin to American audiences?

a. *Julia and Jacques Cooking at Home*

b. *In the Kitchen with Julia and Jacques*

c. *Two French Chefs: Julia and Jacques*

d. *Julia Child's Kitchen, Featuring Jacques Pepin*

Answers to quiz: 1. c; 2. c; 3. a; 4. d; 5. b; 6. d; 7. a; 8. c; 9. b; 10. a

Answers from Match Game: Wells slams Per Se (from page 22):

"swampy mess": mushroom pot pie; "murky and appealing as bong water": matsutake mushroom bouillon; "fat envelopes of pleasure":

Agnolotti with squash; "American playfulness, rigorous finesse": Keller's cooking style; "the oblivious sleepwalking": the service; "limp, dispiriting": yam dumplings; "tasted like peanut butter": chestnut puree; "intransigently chewy": lobster; "heirloom furniture": salmon tartare, oysters in pearls; "hermetic, self-regarding, ungenerous": Per Se itself; "it felt like extortion": eggplant ravioli; "Familiar but transporting": risotto

CHAPTER TWO

Food

A PERSONAL EXPRESSION

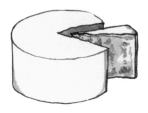

The pleasures of food are social, communal—and personal and individual. "Tell me what you eat," said Brillat-Savarin famously, "and I will tell you who you are." But it's not quite as simple as that, is it? What you eat depends to some degree on where you live. Your personality, family background, food intolerances, health, age, how much money you have in your pocket—all these come into play. It may even depend on what you watch on food television (Giada? Anthony? Paula?). In this chapter we will talk about how food can express who we are while being sure not to neglect all those wickedly fun passions it stirs up as well.

MARCUS SAMUELSSON'S 6 TRUTHS

WHAT HIS STORY CAN TELL US ABOUT OURSELVES AND FOOD

Being a cook and a lover of good food, Marcus Samuelsson has lots of dishes that are meaningful to him. One special dish for him is roast chicken, which his Swedish grandmother taught him how to cook when he was a boy.

Born in Ethiopia. Raised in Sweden. Now the owner-chef of Red Rooster Harlem. Samuelsson's life story has truths and insights for anyone who eats and cooks in today's world—which is, after all, all of us. Here are six of those truths:

1. IT'S A BIG WORLD AND A SMALL PLANET.

Samuelsson grew up in Africa in a time of plague. His birth name is Kassahun Tsegie. When he was a baby, he and his sister contracted tuberculosis. So did his mother, who carried him on her back for miles from their village in the highlands to the capital city of Addis Ababa. Marcus and his sister received treatment at a hospital and survived. His mother did not.

Decades later, after he had become a celebrated chef and television personality, he went back to Ethiopia to rediscover a piece of himself

that had been left behind. (He has since been back many times.) One way he did this was to walk for hours around the Merkato, the open-air market of Addis Ababa, the biggest in Africa, happening upon all sorts of new tastes and spices including a kind of chile powder blend called *berbere*. Berbere is as common in Ethiopia as salt and pepper is here. Returning home, berbere became a favored ingredient of his cooking, not just for what it does to the food but as an expression of his identity, who he is and was.

2. LOVE AND KINDNESS MATTER, IN LIFE AND COOKING.

With Ethiopia beset by civil war and families and children dying from TB and malnutrition, a nurse at the hospital who had saved their lives arranged for Kassahun and Fantaye to be placed with a Swedish adoption agency. This she did with the support and blessing of their dying mother.

At the time, a Swedish couple, Lennart and Anne Marie Samuelsson of Goteborg, were looking to adopt a boy. When they heard about Kassahun, they jumped at the chance to make him part of their family. Since they already had a daughter, they were seeking only a son. But when told the boy had a sister who also needed a home, they took them both. The boy became Marcus, his sister Linda.

Lennart and Anne Marie weren't much into cooking; Marcus's early inspiration came from his grandmother Helga, who grew up in Skane, the gourmet capital of Sweden. Her home, as he recalled in his memoir, was "a little food factory." In it she brought in large cuts of meat and game animals and butchered them. She baked bread. In her basement cellar she made apple and pear jams, pickles, preserved gooseberries and raspberries, pickled onions, cucumbers, beets, and the staple of Swedish cuisine, the herring. Best of all, she invited the

little boy into her factory and her kitchen and showed him how to use the tools and how to cook.

3. FAMILY IS AT THE CORE OF PERSONAL IDENTITY— AND COOKING.

Helga's signature dish was roast chicken, and every time Samuelsson makes it he thinks of her. "The roast chicken I make today is an homage to her. I use perfectly fed chickens, ones that weigh exactly three pounds. My grandmother bought whole chickens from the market, some fat, some skinny. I use real butter instead of fat. But the layering of flavor and the techniques? They're all hers."

When Samuelsson opened Red Rooster, he knew he needed fried chicken on the menu, and although he could prepare a delicious roast chicken in the style of his *mormor*, he had not grown up eating fried chicken like most Americans, so it was hard for him to get it just right. For this he turned to his executive chef Mike Garrett, a one-time dishwasher who teaches at the Institute of Culinary Education in New York. His fried chicken is an homage to family too, *his* family. "You got that aunt who can really cook, it's family reunion time, get your grub on, yummy," as he describes it.

4. WE MARK THE PASSAGES OF OUR LIVES WITH FOOD.

The first meal the young Samuelsson cooked by himself—really all by himself, without his grandmother or mother looking on—occurred when he was twelve, on an Easter trip to the island of Smogen off the west coast of Sweden. It was a guys-only trip: him, his father, and his uncle. They were there to fish and to work, scraping, sanding, and painting the fishing boats to get them ready for summer.

During the trip, Uncle Torsten invited him into the smokehouse where they cured that day's catch of herring and eel. "It was an initiation of sorts, into manhood," he recalled. "Chest puffed up, I stoked the fire, yanked fish off rods, and piled up stones."

The last night they were there, Marcus underwent another initiation of sorts and panfried fish and potatoes for all of them. His father and uncle drank beer and spoke in Swedish dialect, and he reflected with pride on how good the food tasted and the lesson it carried for him. "Although I was still a kid and years away from any thought of becoming a chef, I was learning the beauty of food within a context: how important it is to let the dishes be reflective of your surroundings."

5. FRANCE IS STILL, WELL, FRANCE. IT'S FUNDAMENTAL.

In time Samuelsson moved on from his grandmother's tutelage to learn his trade at restaurants in Sweden and Europe. Eventually he made the pilgrimage to New York, where he landed a job in the kitchen at Aquavit, a small upscale cafe between Park and Madison whose Nordic fusion cuisine seemed a perfect fit for his talents. But he had other things on his mind, notably a stint at the one country he had missed in his travels around Europe. "I had to get to France," he said. "Anyone who wanted to know greatness had to go to France."

Once there he received first-hand lessons in greatness from Georges Blanc at his restaurant in Vonnas, between Dijon and Lyon. His

signature dish was lobster lasagna, made with fresh lobster, sautéed spinach, and oven-dried tomatoes, and it was unlike any lasagna he had ever had before. When Blanc offered him a full-time job, it was, for Samuelsson, like graduating from a culinary academy. He had done what he wanted. He turned down the offer and flew back to New York to carve out his own name in cooking.

6. IT'S A CHARMED LIFE, FOR THOSE OF US FORTUNATE ENOUGH TO LIVE IT.

Back at Aquavit and now in charge of the kitchen, Marcus became the youngest chef ever to win a prestigious 3-star rating from the *Times,* signaling not only his arrival as a chef of prominence but boosting his confidence that he could hang with the heavy hitters in the mostly white, Eurocentric lineup of elite "Division One" chefs—his term—in America's premier restaurant city.

His attractive personality and unique story made him a natural for television, earning him an invitation to compete on Bravo's *Top Chef Masters*. Soon after the show began taping in Los Angeles, he received another invitation—this one from the White House, to oversee President Obama's first state dinner after taking office. That was another hard invite to turn down, and Samuelsson flew back and forth to Washington DC to make sure everything happened as it should. The multicourse dinner included potato and eggplant salad, red lentil soup with fresh cheese, roasted potato dumplings with tomato chutney, green curry prawns with smoked collard greens and coconut-aged basmati, pumpkin pie tart, and chocolate-dipped fruit. The guests of honor—India Prime Minister Manmohan Singh and his wife—were vegetarians.

That done, Samuelsson returned to the cooking show and won it.

CRAIG CLAIBORNE:
FOOD CHAMPION, WORDSMITH

America's food scene a half a century ago looked far different than it does today. Few Americans had ever tried sushi or even knew what it was. People had little interest or appetite for Chinese, Mexican, or Indian food. There were very few fine French and Italian restaurants even in the big cities.

Craig Claiborne helped change all that. Taking over in 1957 as the lead cooking and food writer for the powerful *New York Times*, he used his platform to champion a "palatal revolution"—his term—that has led to a greater appreciation among Americans for new foods, prepared in new ways, from all around the world.

The Mississippi-born and -raised Claiborne, a Southerner to his core despite his home address in the Hamptons (he died in 2000), also had a Southerner's gift for language. A chicken *soong* that began a Chinese dinner one night was "a seraphic first dish." Also inspiring him to look heavenward was the *gigot de poulet* (stuffed chicken leg) from nouvelle cuisine guru Michel Guerard—"a celestial, irresistible creation," he called it.

An author and cook himself, Claiborne was hardly a cheerleader, but if he enjoyed a dish, he could be "enthusiastic in depth" about it. "We must admit," he wrote, "to a keen fancy for all honestly conceived chilies." He admitted as well to taking "undisciplined delight" in ordinary tailgate party fare such as stuffed eggs and sandwiches. Then there was the "awful confession" he had to make to his readers, revealing that steamed clams had not passed between his lips until the ripe old age of twenty-six.

Claiborne saw his role in part as teacher, once offering "a brief discourse" on Greek cooking. His wide travels expanded his palate, and a fish soup he had in Guadalajara remained "so sublimely in the mind" well after he had eaten it. A Vietnamese dish, *pho ga*, instantly "entered our consciousness" after tasting it. Equally consciousness raising was his last bite of a delicious meal, which he described as "an exquisite swallow." Asked what made a good food writer, Claiborne said, "I think you are born with a seed for making a sentence that reads well, as well as one for learning to be discriminating where food is concerned." He had both.

SWEET AND CREAMY

3 MORE LIFE (AND BAKING!) TRUTHS FROM VIOLET CAKES

Claire Ptak is a baker who owns and oversees Violet Cakes, a rough-hewn jewel of a bakery-cafe in the Hackney district of London. Blonde and in her thirties with a sweet smile, she looks every bit the Californian she once was (and may still be in her heart), having grown up in the west Marin foodie village of Point Reyes.

Ptak, also a cookbook author and in-demand food stylist, earned her pedigree as a pastry chef at Alice Waters's Chez Panisse. Her story reveals some solid life and cooking truths as well. Let's cover three of them.

1. LIFE, INCLUDING A LIFE DEVOTED TO FOOD, UNFOLDS IN UNEXPECTED WAYS.

"I never set out to start a bakery," says Ptak, who went to college to study filmmaking. But in between classes she found herself constantly baking and experimenting with new recipes. On a sabbatical in Guatemala she made apple pies for the group of college friends she was traveling with, and one of them described the taste as "Orgasmico!"

Ptak's urge to try different things and go in new directions has not changed over the years—and this quality is revealed in her cooking.

Alice Waters, who tried to talk her into staying at Chez Panisse and not leaving for London, describes her this way: "She is always searching for how to do it better the next time, never relying on the crutch of the familiar and the predictable. That kind of self-inquiry separates a good cook from a great one."

2. TASTE, TASTE, TASTE. THIS IS ESSENTIAL FOR GOOD COOKING.

After college, and after spending some time in go-nowhere jobs in Hollywood and San Francisco, Ptak decided to take a flyer on a one-day internship at Chez Panisse, just to see if she would like working in a restaurant. That one day turned into a three-year gig working with pastry chef Alan Tangren, who learned his trade from Lindsey Shere, Chez Panisse's original, self-taught pastry chef. Tangren taught her the value of simplicity—"He taught me to navigate the line between simplicity and intricacy, and to know when to stop"—and to always taste, taste, taste.

"Each day we baked, tasted, tweaked, and tasted again," she says. "I learned how to taste. We tasted every single thing we made every single day."

SNOB ADVICE

For novices interested in learning "sweet cooking," as Ptak calls it, she recommends starting with ice cream. The reason is that ice cream consists of a basic recipe with eggs and dairy. Then it's a matter of adding flavors according to taste—chocolate, caramel, strawberry, whatever. You make adjustments as you go along based on what you taste, and you learn how such little tweaks can make a big difference in the final result.

3. BALANCE IS EVERYTHING, IN LIFE AND COOKING.

Ptak's chief goal as a baker is to create things that "taste transcendent" and are so good they make people let go of the guilt and worry they have about eating sweets. "It must be worth the calories. Eating cake involves a certain degree of guilt, let's be honest. If you are going to treat yourself, it had better be good, right?"

And yet she wants to do this in a way that honors her values too. She uses organic ingredients such as Madagascan vanilla pods and pure cane molasses, and goes seasonal whenever possible. In the summer when the cherries in Kent are ready, they appear in her whoopee pie icing; the same for those sweet Italian Fragola grapes when they ripen in the fall.

The balance she seeks in her baking was, however, missing from her personal life when she was at Chez Panisse. Turning down an offer of more money and a greater role at the restaurant, Ptak decided to "follow my heart" and chase a dream of love and happiness abroad, going to London to live with her longtime English boyfriend (now husband), Damian. Just as she had when she was in college, she cooked and baked in all her free moments, and she set up a stall at the Broadway Market to sell her pastries.

"I suddenly felt very American," she says about her first day at the big public market in Hackney. "I was so clean and tidy and overeager." Her exuberance stood in sharp contrast to the prim and reserved older British couple who cautiously approached her, quietly inspecting what she had to sell. Finally they ordered a single slice of ginger cake, which they split in two, and left without saying a word.

Then they showed up again the next week and bought another piece of ginger cake, which they split between them just as before. They have been coming back to Ptak's stall week after week for years.

REAL FOODIES

WHO THEY ARE,
HOW TO RECOGNIZE ONE

Claire Ptak is one. So is Marcus Samuelsson. They are food enthusiasts, people who absolutely love to eat, cook, grow in some cases, smell, handle, prepare, gaze adoringly at, take pictures of, shop for, dream of, and endlessly talk about food.

But how do you recognize a real foodie? How do you know when you're in the presence of one? Here are a few tips.

• THEY ARE NOT HAVING CUPCAKES.
Well, they might be; let's qualify that a little. If they are eating cupcakes, they are not doing so with the same gusto they once showed, when cupcakes were in. Cupcakes were once the bomb, but unfortunately for bakers like Ptak, that bomb has gone off.

As she observes, wisely, "Just as our tastes for fashion, design and architecture change, so do our tastes for food. While the cupcake will always be (when made well) the perfectly proportioned marriage of cake and frosting, it is now somewhat out of fashion."

• THEY *ARE* HAVING MILKSHAKES WITH CAKE ON TOP.

Or there could be a lollipop on the top or rock candy or pretzels or a donut or a chocolate chip cookie or a piece of apple pie or whatever—the topping dependent, or not, on the flavor of the shake. Over-the-top milkshakes are what cupcakes once were: the thing you ate (or at least ordered; you don't necessarily have to *eat* it) so you could take a picture of it and post it on social media to show your followers how current you are.

The danger with this approach is that the trends are always changing, and you've got to stay perpetually plugged into the zeitgeist to know what's hot and what's not. Other trends that are dead or on life support: frozen yogurt, boba tea, quinoa, fusion anything, and, yes—bugler, cue the taps—kale.

• THEY CAN TELL YOU THE DIFFERENCE BETWEEN A CRONUT AND A DONUT.

More food trends subject to the whims of the moment are the rainbow bagel, raindrop cake, faro, party brunch, and our favorite for now, the cronut. The cronut is a croissant-donut hybrid that comes in a variety of flavors: rose vanilla, lemon maple, toffee coffee, pumpkin chai, raspberry coconut. It is the invention of New York City baker Dominique Ansel (he has trademarked the name), and his recipe is not simply fried croissant dough; it's more deliciously interesting than that.

Those people you see lined up at all times of the year on Spring Street at seven in the morning a full hour before his shop opens so they can buy their cronuts fresh? Lest there be any doubt, *those are foodies.*

• ANOTHER PLACE YOU CAN SEE THEM: *PORTLANDIA.*

In the brilliant first episode of *Portlandia*, Fred Armisen and Carrie Brownstein play two contemporary food enthusiasts who go to eat

at a Portland cafe. When they ask about the chicken on the menu, the waitress reassures them that it is heritage-bred, woodland-raised, and "fed a diet of sheep's milk, soy, and hazelnuts."

But, Fred wants to know, because this is absolutely vital: "Is it local?"

"Yes, absolutely," says the waitress.

Still, this is not quite enough. Carrie then asks if it's USDA-organic, Oregon-organic, and Portland-organic?

"It's all across the board organic," the waitress replies.

But Fred and Carrie need still more, asking how much space this free-range chicken has to truly roam free. The waitress leaves and returns with the chicken's bio; his name is Colin and there's a color picture of him with his papers. Even this, though, does not placate Fred and Carrie, who decide to personally inspect Colin's former residence on the farm outside the city, asking the waitress to hold their table for them while they're away.

They go to the farm and are gone five years—it's a long story—but when they return to the cafe their table is still waiting for them. Fred and Carrie have changed their minds, however. They'd like the salmon instead.

• THEY LOVE A SHOW.
About the only things missing from the *Portlandia* satire are phones. If Fred and Carrie were real foodies, they would have had their phones with them, snapping selfies and pictures of the crudo with pickled jicama, apples, and beets that they were having with the salmon. Because why? They love a show.

It's dinner theater. But forget the play or magic act that traditionally comprises such entertainment; dinner is the entertainment. It's the play, the magic, the show. And the restaurant is the stage. Chefs have become celebrities, and what their audience demands more than ever—in addition to a beautiful meal—is to be entertained. And if the chef and restaurant succeed in this regard, the feedback is instantaneous and beamed around the world.

"Every night is like opening night," says Ferran Adria, the chef and owner of El Bulli, the defunct Spanish restaurant that was both a gastronomic and entertainment trendsetter. "It has to be magic."

ANTHONY BOURDAIN V. THE WORLD

THE WORLD V. ANTHONY

Anthony Bourdain is a food controversialist, easily the most famous critic and commentator in today's food scene. And he's earned it. As columnist Frank Bruni notes, the chef-turned–television personality has "a tongue on him. It's the sharpest knife in his set."

Bourdain's Sabatier-like tongue has won him many fans and not a few enemies (including Bruni), and several of his most entertaining feuds are outlined here.

ANTHONY V. ALAN RICHMAN

It probably should be noted up front that not all of Bourdain's verbal zingers—precious few, actually—are on a par with Dorothy Parker and the Algonquin Round Table. Some of his remarks shoot for the bottom and somehow strike below it. Such was the case with his put down of food writer Alan Richman. In his book *Medium Raw,* Bourdain entitled a chapter "Alan Richman Is a Douchebag," then refuted his own thesis in that chapter by writing that "Alan Richman is not a douchebag. He's a c*nt."

Richman incurred Bourdain's wrath for, among other things, penning a critical review of Brasserie Les Halles, the Park South restaurant where Bourdain first gained attention as a chef. Bourdain left Les Halles but after the success of *Kitchen Confidential* and his appearances on television, the restaurant named him its "Chef-at-Large." This prompted Richman to do a Patrick Bateman–like dismemberment of Les Halles, which has since shuttered its doors, as a way of attacking Bourdain personally. "He is a living, breathing low blow," Richman says about his nemesis. "That's all he does. He lives it, exults in it, profits from it."

SNOB ASIDE

Without taking sides in the Bourdain v. Richman spat, it is impossible to resist the comment by Chicago food critic Jeff Ruby, who apparently is no fan of Richman's either. Of him he says, "The man's been in so many pissing matches over the years he's got his urologist on speed dial."

ANTHONY V. REGINA

Regina Schrambling is another food writer and a former newspaper food editor who frequently mocks Mario Batali in her blog "Gastropoda." She calls him "Molto Ego," a sly dig on his "Molto Mario" persona and the title of his first Food Network show.

Bourdain, a friend and admirer of Batali's, has called Schrambling "both a hero and a villain" and "easily the Angriest Person Writing About Food" (his capitals). He goes on, "For inventing cute names for her targets, and not having the stones to simply say what everyone knows she is saying, she is a villain. If you're going to piss on Mario every other week, say Mario Batali, not 'Molto Ego.' Stand up f**king proud and tell us why you hate Mario Batali and everything he touches."

ANTHONY V. RUTH BOURDAIN

Schrambling does not save her sarcasm only for Mario; she goes after Anthony too. After he was quoted praising red velvet cupcakes, Schrambling dismissed them as "puke on a page." Their animosity made many in the food world suspect that she was secretly the voice of "Ruth Bourdain," a fictional Twitter creation that combined the names of Bourdain and Ruth Reichl and sent out tweets that parodied the commentary of the two.

For instance, here is an actual Reichl tweet: "Good night. Hot kimchi, slicked w/chiles. Smoky, sweet grilled beef in crisp lettuce. Sake. Slow stroll home down electric streets."

Then came @RuthBourdain, goofing on this tweet: "Bad night. Hot kimchi slicked w/chiles = spicarrhea. Smoking beef in lettuce Zig-Zags laced w/Sake didn't help. Streets electrified by ConEd."

One more. An actual haiku-esque Reichl tweet: "Still. Gray. Cicadas screeching. Such a mournful sound. Fragrant strawberries, just picked. Rivers of yellow cream. Color for a muted day."

Then @RuthBourdain: "Foggy. Stormy. Lightning in the night. Is that asparagus tucked into your softly stirred eggs or are you just happy to see me? Brown butter me."

The gag went on for several years, @RuthBourdain gained seventy thousand followers, and still the writer's identity remained secret. Was it Schrambling? How about restaurant critic Robert Sietsema, who was accused, wrongly, of being the mysterious tweeter? When the James Beard awards presented a humor prize to @RuthBourdain, thinking perhaps that it would smoke him/her out from undercover, it did not work. He/she did not appear at the Manhattan awards ceremony to accept the award, and the buzz about it grew even buzzier.

Turns out it was a he, Josh Friedland, a New Jersey food writer who finally revealed himself because, as he explained, it was either that or "asylum in Venezuela." To avoid being identified he had changed his cell number multiple times, forced the media when interviewing him to sign nondisclosure agreements, and even used software to distort his voice when talking on the phone to reporters.

Both Reichl and Bourdain enjoyed the joke while it lasted, and when Friedland came out, Bourdain tweeted him saying, "It was a good run, well-executed. Stay gold, RB. Stay gold."

ANTHONY V. ALTON BROWN

One of Bourdain's gifts, and it is indeed a gift if you wish to bring attention to yourself and your comments, is being able to pay a compliment to someone while in the same sentence trashing somebody else. So he did with his remark about what television chefs he admired: "I love Ina Garten. She's one of the few people on the Food Network who can actually cook."

Alton Brown, Garten's colleague at the Food Network, rose to the bait. "I don't have to defend my skills against anybody," he said, responding hotly to Bourdain's remark. "I've got 14 years and 252 episodes of a show called *Good Eats* that I'm pretty sure I can use as a resume for my skills." He added, "When was the last time you saw Anthony Bour-

dain actually cook anything? I've spent 14 years cooking my own food on television and I've never seen him cook anything."

Brown softened his criticism by saying that Bourdain was "probably the best writer about food" and a valuable "issue provocateur," words of praise that he has never used to describe Mark Bittman, to our knowledge. Bittman is the influential author of *How to Cook Everything* and a *New York Times* columnist who, in a talk with Ruth Reichl at the 92nd Street Y, criticized food television as "all competition, cleavage and nastiness" and said that he didn't think anyone has "actually learned how to scramble an egg" from watching TV.

Although not mentioned by name, Brown clearly felt the sting, tweeting: "To the thousands who've told me you learned to scramble eggs from *Good Eats*, the shocking truth: You didn't. I guess I should feel grateful that Mark Bittman has excised any illusions I may have had regarding *Good Eats* as a teaching vehicle. Because we know definitively that you can't learn cooking from television. Dang."

Brown, who studied at Vermont's New England Culinary Institute, doesn't like every food program he sees, though. One show he absolutely hated was *Man v. Food*. "That show is about gluttony, and gluttony is wrong. It's wasteful. I think it's an embarrassment," said Brown. *Man v. Food* has since gone out of production and its slimmed down host, Adam Richman, has moved on to other projects.

QUOTABLE SNOB

More from Bourdain. On Las Vegas: "You have to love a town where you can both smoke and gamble in a pharmacy." On writing about food: "Writing incessantly about food is like writing porn. How many adjectives can there be before you repeat yourself?" On the restaurant business: "The greatest business in the world. Cooking is noble toil. It's fun."

ANTHONY V. PAULA DEEN

Of all his food fights, none has stirred more backlash than his attack on Paula Deen, the Southern cook and popular Food Network personality. In a *TV Guide* interview promoting a new season of No Reservations, Bourdain dissed her for the high-caloric food she cooked and how this was contributing to America's problem with obesity. "She revels in unholy connections with evil corporations, and she's proud of the fact that her food is f**king bad for you. I would think twice before telling an already obese nation that it is OK to eat food that is killing us. Plus, her food sucks."

On the off chance someone had missed his point, he beat it with a club, pronouncing Deen "the worst, most dangerous person to America."

Bourdain also delivered swipes at Rachael Ray, Sandra Lee, and Guy Fieri, but only Deen responded, offering a spirited rebuttal. "Anthony Bourdain needs to get a life," she said. "You don't have to like my food, or Rachael's, or Sandra's and Guy's. But it's another thing to attack our character."

Deen said that she and her business partners had fed millions of hungry people by donating meat and food to food banks in the South and elsewhere in the country. She also praised Ray, Lee, and Fieri for their charitable endeavors, in contrast to you know who. "I have no idea what Anthony has done to contribute besides being irritable," she said.

"You know, not everybody can afford to pay $58 for prime rib or $650 for a bottle of wine. My friends and I cook for regular families who worry about feeding their kids and paying the bills." She added that it wasn't that long ago that she was struggling to pay the bills just like them.

Many in the food community who are not fans of Deen nevertheless defended her in the controversy, saying that Bourdain had gone too far. One was Frank Bruni, who described his remarks as "ill-timed elitism" and his "often selective, judgmental and unforgiving worldview." Although he much prefers Bourdain's taste in food over Deen's, Bruni believes that "these preferences reflect privileges and don't entitle me, Bourdain or anyone else who trots the globe and visits ambitious restaurants to look down on food lovers without the resources, opportunity or inclination for that."

As for Bourdain, even he showed mild contrition, clarifying that he had called Deen "the worst, most dangerous cook to America *on the Food Network*," a critical distinction in his mind. He further pledged that if ever asked again about the worst cooks on the Food Network, "I'll just shut up." Probably a good idea, that.

MATCH GAME 2

"WHAT DID HE SAY?" MORE FROM THE MOUTH THAT ROARED

Like our earlier match game with Pete Wells and Per Se, this one requires you to match the comments of Anthony Bourdain on the left with the objects of his disdain on the right. Some of the people mentioned here appear in our nearby companion piece. As in Wells–Per Se, a couple of positive comments are tossed in to keep you on your toes. Answers can be found after the quiz on page 68.

What Anthony said . . .	Who he was talking about
"Those people don't f**king eat. What are they doing writing about food?"	Regina Schrambling
"ewok-like . . . famously inept at cooking (on television)"	James Beard
"Easily the funniest and smartest celebrity chef out there"	Sandra Lee
"Hopelessly, gushily a fan"	Woody Harrelson
"A sh*t film director turned sh*ttier food columnist"	Mario Batali
"By many accounts a complete (if talented and important) bastard"	Gabrielle Hamilton, chef of Prune
"Embittered snarkologist"	Emeril Lagasse
"I look at [person] and I just think, 'Jesus, I'm glad that's not me.'"	Alice Waters
"Pure evil. This frightening Hell spawn of Kathie Lee and Betty Crocker."	Guy Fieri
"Does she even cook anymore? I don't know why she bothers."	Michael Winner
"Why would anyone listen to [person] about anything more important than how . . . to make a bong out of a toilet paper roll and tinfoil?"	Gwyneth Paltrow & Cameron Diaz
"Something very Khmer Rouge about [person] that has become unrealistic."	Rachael Ray

WHO'S THAT TALKING SMACK ABOUT GIADA?

As far as we know, Anthony Bourdain hasn't taken any shots at Giada De Laurentiis, but others certainly have. "Page Six" of the *New York Post* called her "a man-stealing kitchen queen," "one of the few hotties at the stove," and "the food world's first centerfold," among other choice words.

Ah, but that's the *Post*; consider the source. Hey, but wait a minute. Gotham's newspaper of record also fired a broadside at her—sorry, poor choice of words—for how she and other female Food Network stars look on their shows. "Flip through the channels or scan the bookstores and the look is there in all its glory: sort of tight, sort of low-cut, definitely sexy," writes Elaine Louie. "They have thrown away their chef's outfits, aprons and other costumes meant to convey authority and adopted a slightly provocative look instead. It's warm and retro, a bit Marilyn Monroe."

Louie speculates that the look began with British star Nigella Lawson, which Lawson herself has described as "V-necked or scoop-necked, cashmere, three-quarter length sleeves, and very tight and cropped." A New York fashion director labeled it "updated wench chic," saying that the women cooks had to "exude competence but they can't look frowsy. Everyone has to have a little bit of hootchy."

Lawson, Rachael Ray, Cat Cora, Sandra Lee, and De Laurentiis are all singled out for their alleged hootchiness, particularly Giada, whose glamorous movie star looks—she is the granddaughter of the late Italian movie producer Dino De Laurentiis—have rendered her the hootchiest food star in all the land. But Giada, who trained at Le Cordon Bleu, worked at Wolfgang Puck's Spago in Beverly Hills, and has run a successful catering company, heatedly disputes the characterization that what she is doing is food porn, emphasis on the second word.

"Porn? I'm not doing porn!" she responds. "What the hell are people talking about? The way we shot close-ups, I just wanted the food to look beautiful. I thought that's what Americans loved about Italy—that it's so sensual and romantic. [It's not] PBS-style cooking. Lidia Bastianich, sorry, but [she's] kind of boring. I mean, I love Lidia, but you can fall asleep watching her. And Mario Batali? I love Mario to death . . . but he's not romantic or sensual. Those are the things I bring to the table."

She makes a valid argument. Her critics focus on her looks, not her job performance—an all-too-common predicament for women in television and other fields. And who wants to see Mario in a tight-fitting, low-cut cashmere top? That's truly a scary thought indeed.

THE SNOB 10

THE WONDER AND JOY OF PUBLIC MARKETS AND FARMERS' MARKETS

Public markets and farmers' markets are places to go alone or with others, be solitary within a crowd, or engage with people. Whatever your approach, they are a wonder and a joy and a marvel of food and civic life.

When you buy stuff at a farmers' market, you put money directly in the hands of those who are making it or growing it or helping to get it to you—farmers, ranchers, fishermen, truck drivers, laborers, cooks, bakers, butchers, grocers, salespeople, craftspeople of all kinds. There is surely a farmers' market in your area that is worth shopping at. Here are ten markets and their stories.

READING TERMINAL MARKET, PHILADELPHIA

While Boston can claim the honor of holding the first farmers' market in the pre–Revolutionary War colonies, Philadelphia was a close second with its 1693 city charter that designated space for a public market on High Street, later renamed Market Street. This market operated twice a week, farmers and butchers ringing bells on their wagons to let residents in the neighborhood know they were open for business.

Philly's major market today is the Reading Terminal Market. It opened in 1892, and advertised in an early circular that it sold products from

"the truck gardens of New Jersey, the orchards of Pennsylvania, the vineyards of California and the lands of the Tropics." Still boasting a wide array of produce and goods, the market operates in the same basic spot downtown where it has always been. "Cities build and plow under," writes blogger and former newspaper columnist Rick Nichols, a long-time advocate of the market. "Favorite haunts go dark. But the story of the Reading Terminal Market is that it is still with us." ReadingTerminalMarket.org

QUOTABLE SNOB

"Here the thrifty yeomen of Delaware, Chester and Montgomery counties may be seen selling mutton, veal, beef and poultry of their own raising and preparing, 'pound butter,' the product of their own dairies, with all the vegetables and fruits in season fresh from their own gardens and orchards."

—FROM AN 1868 NEWSPAPER ACCOUNT OF PHILADELPHIA'S PUBLIC MARKETS

PIKE PLACE, SEATTLE

Pike Place may be the definitive public market. Founded in 1907 and covering eleven acres of downtown Seattle, it is one of the oldest and biggest in the country. The original Starbucks opened across the street from it in 1971.

A few things to look for when you go: the Oriental Mart, a Filipino market still run by the family that founded it, the Apostols; Alm Hill Gardens, the longest seller of produce at Pike Place in its history; and Rachel, who sits below the neon Public Market sign and clock at the entrance. Rachel is a bronze-cast piggy bank that collects more than ten thousand dollars a year in donations from tourists and others. The funds support a food bank, medical clinic, and senior center in the area. PikePlaceMarket.org

FARMERS MARKET, LOS ANGELES

Besides Hollywood and Vine, the most famous intersection in Southern California is Third and Fairfax in Los Angeles, site of the Farmers Market. In the 1880s it was a dairy farm, owned by the Gilmore family. Oil was discovered, and the dairy cattle quickly gave way to oil wells. The Gilmore Oil Company operated gas stations around the West for decades, and during the Depression they used the property mainly for midget-car racing. Then a couple of entrepreneurs named Fred Beck and Roger Dahlhjelm came up with an idea about what to do about the south parking lot, which was just sitting vacant most of the time.

The Gilmore family agreed to their plan, and on July 14, 1934, a dozen local farmers showed up and sold their fruits and vegetables out of the back of their trucks. A new institution was born. Farmers set up more permanent stalls, restaurants came in—Magee's Kitchen was the first, and it's still there—and Hollywood stars followed. Marilyn Monroe made an appearance as Miss Cheesecake 1953. Nowadays you may spot Jimmy Kimmel shooting segments for his show, or Alton Brown, Gordon Ramsay, Phil Rosenthal, and other television foodies filming episodes there. FarmersMarketLA.com

FERRY PLAZA, SAN FRANCISCO

With so many lovely and colorful things to taste and try—blueberries, peaches, Rose Diamond nectarines, red onions, cantaloupes, portabella mushrooms, Cowgirl Creamery cheese—this farmers' market is a feast for the senses, located as it is at the Ferry Building on San Francisco Bay. The smell of salt is in the air, ships and sailboats move around the waters, foghorns sound, seagulls cackle and scavenge for scraps, and the Bay Bridge looms majestically nearby. For super-fresh seafood, try the Hog Island Oyster Co., whose oyster farm is in Tomales Bay north of the Golden Gate. FerryBuildingMarketplace.com

NASHVILLE FARMERS' MARKET

Even as they stress the values of local produce and supporting local businesses, farmers' markets attract lots of out-of-town visitors who go to shop and sightsee and eat much as they might attend a restaurant or concert or some other attraction in town. So it is with the Nashville Farmers' Market, which is a short, free bus ride from the Ryman Auditorium, Grand Ole Opry, and other storied venues and clubs of Music City. NashvilleFarmersMarket.org

SNOB ASIDE

The Nashville Farmers' Market is on Rosa Parks Boulevard, named after the civil rights pioneer. In her private papers in the Library of Congress, there is a fascinating artifact: a bank deposit slip in which Parks, on the back, scribbled the recipe for what she described as "Featherlite" pancakes. The recipe contained flour, baking powder, egg, and one third of a cup of melted peanut butter, stirred into the batter. She reminded herself to "combine with dry ingredients [and] cook at 275° on griddle."

BOSTON PUBLIC MARKET

Although the tradition of farmers bringing their crops to market in Boston dates back centuries, the indoor Boston Public Market is of relatively recent vintage, having been established in the early 2000s at the Haymarket station of the T, the city's subway system. It's year-round, and everything sold there is from Massachusetts or New England. One spot to check out is the thirty-two-hundred-square-foot kitchen where they hold cooking demos and other food programs.

While you're there, strike up a conversation with someone; the *New Republic's* Corby Kummer would like that. "As any regular farmers' market visitor knows, a good market is about more than buying

food," he writes. "It's about striking up conversations, exchanging information, feeling part of a community and actively contributing to it." BostonPublicMarket.org

UNION SQUARE GREENMARKET, NEW YORK CITY

One of the most attractive aspects of the Union Square Greenmarket and other public markets is hidden in plain sight: It's free. There's no admission fee; anyone can walk in. "Union Square," says blogger Alexander Kaufman, "is one of those rare places left in Manhattan where just about anyone has business being." This being Manhattan, market days are huge, attracting tens of thousands of eaters and shoppers. GrowNYC.org

DANE COUNTY FARMERS' MARKET, MADISON

The Dane County Farmers' Market of Madison, Wisconsin, sees its role in very simple terms: "to unite the urban and rural cultures." It has been doing so since the early 1970s, when only five farmers showed up to sell produce on it first day of business. By the next year, though, urban and rural folks had warmed to the idea and it has since become a Madison institution. Its open-air setting on the Capitol Mall in front of the Capitol building is lovely. DCFM.org

EASTERN MARKET, WASHINGTON, DC

Of the scores of farmers' markets to choose from in and around DC, try the Eastern Market, an indoor and outdoor market in the Capitol Hill neighborhood of the city. The beautifully restored nineteenth-century North Hall serves as the indoor venue for the produce, seafood, meat, and flower vendors. On the plaza outside the hall and on surrounding streets are painters, woodworkers, potters, and other craftspeople. EasternMarket-DC.org

GREEN CITY MARKET, CHICAGO

The Green City Market came into being largely because of Abby Mandel Meyer, a cookbook author and columnist whose enthusiasm for good food began when she saw Julia Child do a cooking demo. Her dream was to create a farmers' market in Chicago similar to the ones she had visited in France. Wholly devoted to natural foods, she insisted that the market sell only fruits and vegetables produced by local farmers using green agricultural practices.

Meyer died of cancer a decade ago but lived long enough to see her creation grow into a treasured city and regional gathering held in the south end of Lincoln Park and at the Notebaert Nature Museum. Alice Waters, who knows a thing or two about farm-fresh produce, has called Green City "the best sustainable market in the country." GreenCityMarket.org

FOODIE SNOB QUIZ #2
MUSIC AND THE FOOD OF LOVE

"If music be the food of love, play on," wrote Shakespeare, who kindly provided the inspiration for this chapter's quiz: love songs with food references or themes.

These songs may also serve as songs to cook by, and as mood music for when the cooking and eating are over, and you and your love retire to a cozy spot on the sofa in front of the fire and other activities commence. Answers to this eclectic hit parade follow.

1. In Dean Martin's endearing "That's Amore," he sings about how "the moon hits your eye like a big pizza pie," pasta "fazool," and drinking wine. The song, the theme for the equally endearing romantic comedy *Moonstruck*, talks about a city in Italy where "love is king." What's the city?
   a. Roma
   b. Napoli
   c. Firenze
   d. Venezia

2. The writer Michael D'Alimonte gripes that Jack Johnson's easy-listening hit, "Banana Pancakes," forced all guys like him to get up and make banana pancakes for their girlfriends. In it Johnson asks the girl to stay in bed where they are and ignore what bothersome intrusion?
   a. dog that needs to be let outside
   b. FedEx delivery at the door
   c. a ringing phone
   d. a car alarm

3. Especially when topped by cream, peaches serve as a metaphor for love and sex in pop music. One example is "Peaches 'n' Cream," a thumping, Luther Vandross-style R&B groove recorded by an artist known for his love of the high life. (Note his drinking song "Gin & Juice.")
   a. Ziggy Marley
   b. Snoop Dogg
   c. Keith Richards
   d. Bruno Mars

4. Another pop song replete with sexual innuendo is the Supremes' "Buttered Popcorn." Florence Ballard—not Diana Ross—sings lead, saying how her man wants "more butter, more butter, more butter" all the time. This recalls a quote by a legendary chef who famously wanted "butter, butter, butter! Give me more butter!" Who was the chef?

   a. Fernand Point
   b. Auguste Gusteau
   c. Escoffier
   d. Julia Child

5. Cole Porter's classic "You're the Top" is a sly and sexy number that a man sings to a woman or they sing as a duet—he's the bottom, as the lyrics go, and she's the top! The song lists several food items as being the top, the best, like the girl being sung about. One, believe it or not, is broccoli. Which one of these items is NOT listed in the song?

   a. hot tamale
   b. turkey dinner
   c. wedding cake
   d. Ovaltine

6. In another duet from the Great American songbook, Fred Astaire and Ginger Rogers sing Ira Gershwin's "Let's Call the Whole Thing Off," in which they quibble about how to pronounce certain words, such as "to-may-to" and "to-mah-to." What other food or foods do they disagree on? More than one answer is acceptable.

   a. potato
   b. banana
   c. oyster
   d. They disagree on all three.

7. The Newbeats's pop hit "Bread and Butter" is a love and breakup song. In it the guy sings falsetto about how his girl "don't cook mashed potatoes, she don't cook T-bone steak"—no, no, no, she makes him bread, butter, toast, and jam because that's what he likes. Then he comes home one night, and his girlfriend is cooking up something *different* for another guy. What classic Southern meal is she making him?

  a. chicken and dumplings
  b. collard greens
  c. steak, potatoes, and peas
  d. biscuits and gravy

8. The opening number of the musical *Oliver!*—words and music by Lionel Bart—is a love song of a different sort: to food. In "Food Glorious Food," the boys in a London orphanage sing of the joys of "hot ___ and mustard, cold jelly and custard." What food are the boys longing for?

  a. porridge
  b. sausage
  c. turkey
  d. rashers

9. Another musical, another unusual love song—this one involving a boy, his dog, and supper. The dog is Snoopy, the musical is *You're a Good Man, Charlie Brown*, and the song is "Suppertime." In it Snoopy tells Charlie to "bring on the soup dish, bring on the cup, bring on the ____, and fill me up." What does Snoopy want?

  a. a. bone
  b. b. hamburg (without "er")
  c. c. kibbles
  d. d. bacon

10. The death of Prince in 2016 deprived the music world of one of its most creative spirits—and one who made frequent food references in his songs, such as the cherry pie and apple kisses in "Good Love" and the mango, nectarine, and honeydew in "Soul Sanctuary." In "Let's Go Crazy," one of his all-time greats, what color is the banana he makes sexual allusions to?

   a. purple

   b. yellow

   c. blue

   d. brown

Answers: 1. b; 2. c; 3. b; 4. a; 5. c; 6. d; 7. a; 8. b; 9. d; 10. a

Answers to Match Game 2 on page 57: More from the Mouth That Roared

"Those people don't eat": Paltrow & Diaz; "ewok-like": Emeril Lagasse; "Easily the funniest": Mario Batali; "Hopelessly, gushily": Gabrielle Hamilton; "A sh*t film director": Michael Winner; "By many accounts": James Beard; "embittered snarkologist": Regina Schrambling; "I look at [person]": Guy Fieri; "Pure evil": Sandra Lee; "Does she even cook": Rachael Ray; "Why would anyone listen": Woody Harrelson; "Something very Khmer": Alice Waters.

CHAPTER THREE

It's a matter of taste

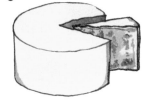

"What is food to one," said Lucretius, "is to others bitter poison." We moderns would express this sentiment more directly: Taste is subjective. But in this age of social media, in which anyone can post opinions about just about anything and develop a wide audience, does taste even matter anymore? Well, yes, it does. If you blow the pronunciation of haricot verts (*are-ee-coe-verr*) at a dinner party, the woman seated across from you with the Che Guevara tattoo on her bare upper arm may secretly cast you as a member of Mencken's Booboisie, and who wants that? References to Lucretius, Che, and Mencken in a single paragraph—get ready for a *very* tasty chapter.

WHAT THE 60-MINUTE GOURMET THINKS

A TASTEFUL DISCUSSION OF GOOD TASTE

One could do worse in matters of taste than to defer to Pierre Franey, who was, in his time, one of America's leading culinary tastemakers, the chef of the best French restaurant in the country and the author of a popular and influential cooking column, "60 Minute Gourmet," for the *New York Times*.

In A. A. Milne's delightful poem "The King's Breakfast," the King explains to his subjects that he's not a fussy man; all he would like is "a little bit of butter to my bread." Franey was like that king; not a fussy man, but one with clear standards of excellence informed by his experience, training, and judgment—the perfect person to lead a discussion on what constitutes "one of the most subjective things on earth": good taste.

GOOD TASTE IS NOT A MATTER OF PUTTING ON AIRS.
If you've ever been to Paris and been mocked by a clerk at a patisserie for your attempts to speak French, it's understandable if one associates fine French food with expressions of aristocratic disdain. This was not Franey, though.

Born in Burgundy, he loved cooking and food so much as a boy—his nickname was Pierre Le Gourmand—that his family sent him to Paris at the age of thirteen to apprentice at restaurants. He did drudge work in the kitchens, without pay, and over time landed a paying job at Drouant, one of the city's best restaurants, preparing the fish. One evening a sous chef decided to test him by ordering him to make an omelet. When the teenager nervously moved the pan too much, the chef smacked him in the side of the head with a spatula, at which point Franey threw the omelet in the chef's face and ran out of the kitchen.

The chef apologized and Franey returned to his post, and his stature at Drouant rose after the incident. Though young, Pierre Le Gourmand was clearly someone who would not be bullied by others, who trusted his own mind, who knew—if you gave him the space—how to cook an omelet. "All it takes," he said, "is a decent pan, fresh eggs and a good dash of self confidence."

GOOD TASTE IS BEING OPEN TO ALL KINDS OF FOOD.

Franey came to this country for the first time in 1939, working as an assistant fish chef for the French pavilion at the New York World's Fair. After the fair closed, Henri Soulé, the *maître d'hotel* in charge of the pavilion, decided to open a French restaurant in New York City, aptly named Le Pavillon. His *chef poissonnier* was Franey, who was twenty-one.

Then came Pearl Harbor, and the arc of his life abruptly changed. After joining the US Army, he turned down an assignment to be General Douglas MacArthur's personal chef, instead choosing to go overseas and fight to liberate France and the rest of Europe. That he did, earning a Purple Heart after being wounded in combat.

When the war ended, Franey came back to his adopted country, resumed working at Le Pavillon (now as executive chef), and came

to know American cuisine for all its strengths and weaknesses. One staple of that cuisine, hamburger dishes and other dishes made with ground meats, he viewed with an open mind despite its lowly status among gourmands.

"Many Americans seem to look with disdain on dishes made with ground meats, relegating them to a low position in the hierarchy of foods," he said. But he wasn't sure why. Many nations, not just the United States, favor ground-meat dishes. The hamburger, he speculated, may originally have been of Russian origin; the Slavic words *bitok* or *bitoke*, when translated into English, meant "beefsteak."

Similarly, he did not understand why some turned their noses up at so-called "peasant food" such as sausages. "In the hierarchy of food there is no doubt that sausages are what could be called food for the masses or a peasant concept," adding that he had yet to meet a lover of fine foods who did not eat and enjoy grilled pork sausages, served perhaps at a picnic or tailgate party with a potato salad on the side.

SNOB ASIDE

It's a throwaway line, and you'll miss it if you're not paying attention, but in the funny old-time romantic comedy *Desk Set*, Joan Blondell refers quickly to Franey's (and Henri Soulé's) grand French restaurant in New York City, saying to Katharine Hepburn as she's waiting to be picked up for lunch by Spencer Tracy: "If he takes you to Pavillon, try the chicken with truffles. It's marvelous."

GOOD TASTE IS NOT A MATTER OF BEING A PURIST.

This was a constant theme of Franey's; he was very clear about it. Good taste is not dogmatism or pedantry or purism.

"It is as amusing as it is astonishing how deeply exercised 'food enthusiasts' can become over one recipe over another," he wrote.

"That is not to say that I will abide transgressions against classic French cooking and will not make my protests about misnomers in the name of Escoffier as loud as possible. What I have in mind are the supposed 'purists' who are opposed to variances from what their palates are accustomed to."

One expression of purism he found absurd was the prohibition about sauce on fresh scallops; in this mindset they can only be broiled or sautéed, no other way permitted. His view, on the other hand, was that changing things up with a nice wine or cream sauce can be very nice.

Another silly notion pushed by the purists of his time was that berries and fruit were only for breakfast or at the end of a meal, and they could never be combined with poultry, fish, or meat. If this is so, he asked, how does one explain such delicious French classics as duck á l'orange or Véronique (sole with grapes)?

GOOD TASTE APPRECIATES SIMPLICITY, WHEN DONE WELL.

Franey became a hero to home cooks everywhere with his "60-Minute Gourmet" columns, which were collected into two best-selling books. Long before anyone had ever heard of the term "fast casual," Franey's recipes (with an assist from Craig Claiborne) demonstrated how you could make delicious food relatively quickly and on a budget. Key to his methods and unfussy philosophy was another idea: Complicated is not necessarily better.

"There is a prevailing notion that, with the exception of dishes like salade nicoise and céleri rémoulade, all the dishes that go from stove burner to table top are intricately involved, endlessly complicated dishes, any of which requires the better part of a day and night to bring to the proper state of perfection. It simply isn't true."

**GOOD TASTE IS NOT STATIC; IT'S A PROCESS
OF CONSTANT LEARNING.**

On this, for all his seventy-five years—Franey died in 1996; his family grows and maintains herbs at his gravesite on Long Island—he remained resolute. One is not born to good taste; nor does one arrive at it as if at the top of a mountain and therefore has no need to do anything more. It is rather an adventure, a continual process of growing and learning; that's what good taste was to him.

"I find myself rarely bored by cooking," he recalled as an older man. "It was an adventure for me when I was an apprentice and it is an adventure now that all the young chefs start to look more and more like children."

And, one final thought: "What is a gourmet dish? To my mind a gourmet dish is any food prepared with a mixture of conscience, care and intelligence." Those last three words also serve as an apt description of Franey himself.

LE SNOB HUIT

8 FRENCH FOODIES YOU ABSOLUTELY MUST KNOW FOR YOUR NEXT DINNER PARTY

France no longer dominates haute cuisine the way it once did. More and more people are recognizing that a host of countries around the

world—Italy of course, China, Japan, Thailand, Vietnam, India, Mexico, Brazil, South Africa, the Nordics—have extraordinary national cuisines that are pretty haute too.

Still, one would be hard-pressed to host a dinner party of foodies and not have French cuisine be a topic of discussion during the evening. Here, then, is a guide to famous chefs and foodies of the Gallic past; feel free to drop their names into the conversation and impress and outdo others with your dazzling displays of arcana.

MARCEL PROUST

A great conversation starter at a dinner party is to ask about a person's "madeleine moment," a special memory he or she has about food. The phrase originates from a story about Proust—how he dipped a madeleine cookie into a cup of tea, took a bite of it, and the emotion he felt in that moment so transported him that it touched the deepest part of his psyche and unleashed a torrent of memories in him that propelled him to write, over the course of many years, the literary masterwork once known as *Remembrance of Things Past* but now more popularly translated as *In Search of Lost Time*.

If that last sentence seems somewhat long and tortured, well, it's a pretty long and tortured book too. The Proust epic is in fact seven books, covering about three thousand pages, which means that no one but no one at your dinner party will have read the whole thing, or probably even a piece of it, or frankly, not even a word of it. *In Search of Lost Time* fits the Twain definition of a classic: a book everyone admires but no one reads. And in the extremely unlikely event there is someone at your party who has actually read the first volume, *Swann's Way*, and not the CliffsNotes version of it way back in a college lit class, he will no doubt have discovered something that food people, for whatever reason, would prefer not to admit.

It's not about madeleines. It's not about madeleines at all. Like a lot of Frenchmen, Proust spent a lot of time in bed, only in his case he was able to make a career out of it. But he wasn't a food writer; he had other things on his mind. Art, death, the nature of life—these were his chief themes, not pastry.

"The Proust madeleine phenomenon is now as firmly established in folklore as Newton's apple or Watt's steam kettle," groused the old-time *New Yorker* writer A. J. Liebling, who knew about such things and who summarized the phenomenon thusly, "The man ate a tea biscuit, the taste evoked memories, he wrote a book."

The madeleine passage buried deep in Proust's literary basement is one paragraph long and totals 58 words; and yet many would like to believe that it was so powerful and profound it caused him to spit out another 2,942 words. The sharp-eyed Liebling didn't buy any of it; here's his 3-word take on Proust's writing formula (and the formula of food writers and cookbook authors today):

Taste > Memory > Book

Liebling looked up the madeleine recipe in *Larousse*—"a light cake made with sugar, flour, lemon juice, brandy and eggs"—and he was skeptical about that too, particularly the amount of alcohol called for. "The quantity of brandy in a madeleine would not furnish a gnat with an alcohol rub," he sniffed.

Liebling wrote those words decades and decades ago, but it's a safe bet that decades and decades from now, the foodies of the future will be sitting around the table at a dinner party and someone will ask about their "madeleine moments." So go ahead. Maybe even serve them for dessert.

QUOTABLE SNOB

FERNAND POINT

Lording over his realm, the restaurant La Pyramide in Vienne near Lyon, Chef Point was a demanding perfectionist who insisted on only the best—Baccarat crystal, Limoges porcelain, and the freshest produce shipped in by train every day from Les Halles market in Paris. "I'm not hard to please," he said in a statement that epitomized his philosophy. "I'm content with the very best."

He was also a rebel. Unafraid to challenge tradition if he did not see the sense of it, the mustachioed Point (he resembled a slimmed down version of Auguste Gusteau in *Ratatouille*) broke longstanding French custom by leaving the kitchen and speaking with his guests at their tables in the dining room, asking them what they would like and fixing it for them. This was simply not done until Point did it. Chefs in those days were hired help; they stayed in the back, not seen, not heard from.

But his guests had to be on their best behavior when he entered the room! Yes, Chef! It is said that he once threw a party of four out of La Pyramide because one of the men at the table was holding his champagne glass by the bowl, not the stem. This was unforgivable because the drink had been served at the ideal temperature, and

Point could not abide the thought of the man warming it up with his hand and wrecking the perfection of the moment.

If things get off schedule at your dinner party and you are a tad late in getting dinner on the table, consider channeling Point and delivering one of his most famous lines: "La grand cuisine must not wait for the guest. It is the guest who must wait for la grand cuisine!"

PAUL BOCUSE

Bocuse trained under Point, who required him to make *gratin de queues d'écrivesses* every day for two years before Point would consider serving it at his restaurant. But Bocuse clearly learned his lessons well, because he was, according to Craig Claiborne, "almost indisputably the most famous chef in the world" when he came to New York City in 1975 to open his restaurant Le Colisee on East 60th. How indisputably famous was he? Pierre Franey and Jacques Pepin assisted him in the kitchen.

Bocuse's favorite English word then was *impeccable*, which he used several times to describe the dishes he, Franey, and Pepin served at the opening. Not so impeccable were his thoughts on why there were so few women chefs at the highest levels of cuisine. "Women lack the instincts for great cooking," he told Claiborne. "Women who become chefs are limited in their accomplishments. They have one or two dishes they accomplish very well but they are not great innovators."

Ouch! It may be best to steer your guests away from such topics, unless you're looking to sow dissension and friction—typically not a recipe for a successful dinner party. While a restaurant kitchen remains an intense, testosterone-charged setting that is often hostile to the presence of women, the world has changed considerably since then and Bocuse's views in this regard surely have evolved too. What has not changed is his passion for fine food. Auberge du Pont de Col-

"Let Paris live in your soul, in your kitchen, and in your home every day of the year," said Patricia Wells, the New York food writer and author who moved to Paris in the early 1980s to begin her culinary explorations of the city. When she ate a dish at a fine restaurant, she tried to reproduce it back in the kitchen of her flat. Her books, notably *The Food Lover's Guide to Paris*, introduced Americans to the world's greatest city before the age of the Internet, and its updated fifth edition is still a valuable go-to resource.

longes, his restaurant near Lyon, earned a Michelin three-star rating in 1965 and has maintained this rating every year since.

ESCOFFIER

Escoffier is "the father of modern French cooking" (Jeremiah Tower) or "the Moses of French cookery" (Pierre Franey): Either way, he's so big that, like Beyonce or Rihanna, he's referred to only by one name. Here's a trivia question for your party: What is his first name? Fittingly, considering his stature as a Biblical prophet of French cuisine, he had two of them: George Auguste.

Stories of Escoffier abound; most tend to illustrate his high and exacting standards. Here are two.

A wealthy American woman asked him once to make turkey with oyster stuffing for a Thanksgiving meal she was having at the Hotel Ritz in Paris, where he was chef and grand master. Escoffier went ballistic, saying no, absolutely not, one never paired oysters with turkey or fowl of any kind and the thought of it was abhorrent and "cannibalistic." Needless to say, the woman had something else for Thanksgiving.

And: The Australian opera singer Nellie Melba was singing at Covent Garden in London, and Escoffier, a huge opera buff, made her

dinner one night at the Savoy Hotel, where he also presided during his extraordinary career. To surprise her, he created a magnificent dessert with peaches and vanilla ice cream served in a metal dish and presented between the wings of a swan carved out of ice and frosted with sugar. Later Escoffier tweaked the dessert and served it at the Savoy, changing the ice cream to raspberry and inventing what we know today as the peach Melba.

BRILLAT-SAVARIN

The author of the famous quote about how you are what you eat, this nineteenth-century food writer and philosopher has a cheese named after him, perhaps the highest honor a Frenchman can achieve. Paul Baudelaire, the poet, was no fan however, knocking him as "a man of great renown who was at the same time a great fool, two things that go very well together." The French gourmand Gerard Oberle was another hater, attacking his greatest work, the *Physiology of Taste*, as "a bogus masterpiece."

For contemporary eaters, one of Brillat-Savarin's most memorable achievements occurred in 1798 in an incident he describes in his book. At the palace of Versailles one day he and a government officer, Monsieur Laperte, sat down to have a few oysters for lunch. A few? Try a mountain. They started with a dozen apiece, then went to two dozen, then three, at which point Brillat-Savarin begged off, letting Monsieur Laperte go boldly where no man had gone before. Over the next hour he ate a mind-boggling and stomach-churning— it's not a typo—32 *dozen* oysters. Brillat-Savarin noted apologetically that his companion would have finished in less time except that "the servant was not very skillful at opening them."

Another name-game trivia question for your guests: What was Brillat-Savarin's first name? Jean-Anthelme.

Although Gerard Oberle, in classic food writerly fashion, resented his rival Brillat-Savarin, he was a true Frenchman in the sense that he hated oatmeal for breakfast. Once he was visiting an American friend who set a bowl of oatmeal in front of him in the morning. With a pained expression he pushed it away and refused to eat it, saying, "Why do you begin the day with punishment?"

NAPOLEON

When the dinner party conversation turns to the subject of "megalomaniacal dictators who had sublime taste in food," one name will of course come to the fore: the inspiration for Napoleon brandy and Napoleon the pastry.

Here is a Napoleon anecdote that will regale the guests.

The year is 1800. The once hope for democracy, soon to be tyrannical emperor of France has just defeated the Austrians in a climactic battle near the village of Marengo in Italy. To honor this achievement, Napoleon's chef, a man named Dunand, sends his team out into the countryside to gather the raw materials for that evening's celebratory feast. They bring back chickens, eggs, tomatoes, garlic, olive oil, a skillet from a farmhouse kitchen, and crayfish they caught in a stream. Using all that is available to him, the masterful Dunand cooks the chicken in oil; adds tomatoes, water, and garlic; steams the crayfish; and fries the eggs for garnish. Afterward Napoleon declares it to be the best dinner he's ever had, and Dunand's creation, first known as chicken Marengo, evolves over time into the classic French dish: chicken a la Provençal.

HENRI QUATRE

If your guests enjoyed your Napoleon anecdote, here is another vintage chicken story they may like as well.

This one centers on King Henri IV of France, not to be confused with King Henry IV of England. The former spelled his name with an *i* and reigned in the late 1500s and early 1600s, while the latter spelled his name with a *y* and ruled a couple of centuries earlier. Your guests may not know, or care, about the difference between the two Henrys, although if there is a French national at the table, he or she surely will. It is a point of pride to the French that it was Henri IV who declared, "I want there to be no peasant in my kingdom to be so poor that he cannot have a chicken in his pot every Sunday."

"A chicken in every pot" may not seem like much by today's gastronomic standards, but in its time it was an extraordinary act: a king delivering an order from the throne, and then acting upon it, to benefit the lowliest of society. Henri IV's subjects viewed him with great affection, calling him *Le Vert Gallant* ("The Gay Old Spark") for his grand sexual exploits with women—another much-admired attribute of the French.

Presidents and other American politicians running for office later appropriated this phrase, also promising a chicken in every pot and in the early days of the automobile, adding "a car in every garage" to it. Both expressions were meant to evoke prosperity.

BATTLE OF THE CLASSIC CUISINES

FRENCH V. ITALIAN: WHICH IS BETTER?

It is said that Catherine de Medici, the daughter of an Italian noble family, brought recipes from Italy when she married King Henri II of France and ascended to the throne as queen in the 1500s. This, according to the story, is how the great food and culinary traditions of France began.

True or not, this story goes straight to the heart of an enduring foodie debate: Whose cuisine is better, French or Italian? Here's your chance to decide once and for all. Note the categories on the left, the French and Italian contenders for each, and our choice as the winner on the right. See if your picks agree with ours in this determinedly capricious and whimsical battle of the classic cuisines.

Category	French	Italian	Winner
Most romantic food city	Paris	Venice	Paris
Most romantic dish	Soufflé	Risotto	Risotto
Sexiest celebrity chef	Eric Ripert	Giada De Laurentiis	Giada De Laurentiis
Comfort food	Cassoulet	Lasagne alla Bolognese	Lasagne alla Bolognese
Specialty food	Truffles	Balsamic vinegar	Truffles
Most capacious eater & drinker	Gerard Depardieu	Mario Batali	Mario Batali
Drink to celebrate with	Champagne	Prosecco	Champagne
Big reds	Burgundy/Bordeaux	Brunello/Amarone	Burgundy/Bordeaux
Cheese varieties	600-plus	300-plus	France
Old school dessert	Pots de crème	Tiramisu	Tiramisu
Coffee & pastry	Café au lait & croissant	Cappucino & biscotti	Tie
Best food movie inspired by its cuisine	Ratatouille	Big Night	Ratatouille
Most World Cups	1	4	Italy
Favorite food book	Foodie Snob	Foodie Snob	Tie

Final result: It's a tie! France 6, Italy 6, with two ties. Both cuisines are truly epic. Not only that, Kevin Nelson's *Foodie Snob* is the literary choice of both French and Italian food enthusiasts, a sure sign of impeccable taste.

JIM HARRISON, AMERICAN ORIGINAL

For an American perspective, let us turn to the man Mario Batali called "the Homer, the Michelangelo, the Lamborghini, the Willie Mays, the Secretariat of words." He was no wimpy madeleine eater either.

His name was Jim Harrison, and while writing *Legends of the Fall* and other acclaimed stories and novels, he was eating. A lot. "It is my private opinion that many of our failures in politics, art and domestic life come from our failure to eat vividly," wrote Harrison, who never failed in that respect.

He once ate a thirty-seven-course, nineteen-wine meal in France that began at lunch and ended after midnight. At a poker game one night he snacked on the hearts of five deer that he and his friends had shot hunting in the woods of Michigan's Upper Penin-sula where he lived. Another time, in the spirit of Brillat-Savarin and Laperte, he downed twelve dozen oysters in a sitting. Such exploits naturally drew criticism as being too much of a good thing, criticism he dismissed as emanating from "food bullies" and "health bores" whose holier-than-thou edicts robbed joy from eating and cooking, both realms in which he excelled.

"Small portions are for smallish and inactive people," he said. And: "My notion, scarcely original, is that if you eat badly you are probably living badly." But eating well for him was not necessarily eating rich. "At odd times I still love spaghetti and meatballs," he confided. "It is soul food, a balm, a food nostrum that helps me understand the often questionable arc of my life." That arc ended in 2016 after seventy-eight full years.

HOW TO READ A MENU
7 INSIGHTS FROM JEREMIAH TOWER

A menu is a menu is a menu. So most people think.

Jeremiah Tower is not most people. The former Tavern on the Green chef and past chef-owner of Stars in San Francisco, a mentor of Mario Batali, the daring innovator who (along with his ex-boss, Alice Waters) helped create California Cuisine, he sees menus as "a language unto themselves" that are far more than a simple recitation of the items the restaurant is serving that day.

Here are seven insights from Tower on what you're really looking at when you look at a menu.

1. MENUS ARE, AT THEIR MOST IMAGINATIVE AND EVOCATIVE, AN EXPRESSION OF FANTASY.

This is how Tower sees them, and this was how he saw them as a boy, growing up in Australia when he collected menus the way other children collect baseball cards or Barbie dolls. The menus created a picture of a world in his mind, a world far away from his, and he would imagine not just the food that was being served, but also the people who were eating it, how they were dressed, how the tables were set, what the staff said and did, and the ambience of the evening.

"They spoke to me as clearly as any childhood fantasy novel," he recalls. "Reading an old menu slowly forms in my mind's eye its era, the sensibility of the restaurateur or the chef, even the physical details of the dining room. I can picture the guests even when I don't know who they were."

2. MENUS CAN EVOKE THE PAST AND STIR MEMORIES.

Tower's biggest influence when he was young was his mother Margaret, who taught him to cook and garden and who hosted garden parties at their home in a Sydney suburb. "When I think again about one of my mother's summer garden party menus, the whole day is conjured up—mayonnaise-covered poached whole salmons laid out in the tents. I can see everyone who was there."

Inspired by his early days with his mother, Tower pioneered the use of edible flowers in salads and other dishes, a trend not everyone enjoyed. One time he was conducting a cooking demo with Joan Lunden on *Good Morning America*, and he put blossoms into the salad he was making for her. She was not pleased, however. "I hate flowers," Lunden said, and immediately cut to a commercial break.

SNOB ADVICE

Those like Jeremiah Tower who appreciate old menus will enjoy the extraordinary online menu collection of the Los Angeles Public Library. It's a searchable database of historic menus from Los Angeles and nearby cities; it includes restaurants, steamships, airlines, and banquets. See an image and details from the actual menu of say, Hollywood's Brown Derby, then imagine Bogie and Bacall sitting down at a table to order a Cobb salad. Lapl.org

3. A MENU IS AN INVITATION TO BROADEN YOUR PALETTE.

Tower researched old menus partly for pleasure, partly for career reasons (he would re-create dishes he saw on them), and partly to broaden his palette. If he saw something exquisite being served somewhere, he would make a mental note—or a physical one; he kept detailed notebooks on what he ate and the meals he cooked—to try that himself someday.

One menu he cherished—by this time he had said good-bye to Australia and was in Cambridge going to Harvard—was one he discovered while reading a Lord Peter Wimsey detective story by Dorothy L. Sayers. The menu featured a Château Lafite vintage 1875 during the *poulet* course and an ancient imperial Tokay with dessert, instilling in him the desire to taste both an old Lafite and the Tokay. This he did many years later—the Hungarian wine when he was working at Chez Panisse, and then after that, across the bay at his restaurant Stars, when he held a West Coast tasting of old Lafites. One of the highlights of this event for him was uncorking an 1875.

4. MENUS ARE A REFLECTION OF THEIR TIME—AND YOURS.

Here are two examples of this, although there are many.

Sir Cecil Beaton was a brilliant photographer, a sharp-dressed man, and the costume and set designer for the exquisitely beautiful Broadway musical *My Fair Lady* (he also did costumes and sets for the movie). In the late 1960s Beaton hosted a grand fête in Paris at Lapérouse for a dozen of his closest male friends and him. The meal included the "fat of a turtle" served with Chateau d'Yquem 1860, cold foie gras, and truffles poached in champagne. Tower found (and kept) the menu for that evening, and although it seemed a bit, ah, over the top for his tastes, he could not help but reflect on how different his life was from Beaton's.

Jump to Tower, living the '60s stoner college life in Cambridge and, as always, cooking up meals and menus. One he described as "a self-consciously decadent menu"; it included homemade buffalo grass-flavored vodka and consommé marijuana, a soup-like drink that he concocted from pot plants with the stems soaked in chicken stock. He made this brew for two friends and a Boston poet he was interested in, but none of them actually got high from it, Tower included, because it took too long for the dope to get to their heads, and by then they had already moved on to a dessert of strawberries and cream and were pouring a California Korbel Brut.

5. A MENU SHOWS MOVEMENT AND PROGRESSION.

As static as the words may appear on the page, a menu tells a story of movement just like a good book or magazine article. The best menus, for Tower, are perfect in "language, balance and progression of food." It is not just what is being served, the ingredients and so forth, but the statement of the dishes, in words. The words ought to reflect what is being served. Some chefs today are menu mini-malists, using only a phrase or a cleverly suggestive title to convey the essence of the dish. This is in reaction to the more traditional approach that lists the various ingredients.

Growing older and more serious about the food he wished to make, Tower fell under the influence of Richard Olney, the Iowa-born writer, painter, and cook who moved to France, grew enraptured with French country cooking and the abundant simplicity of it, and wrote two cookbooks, *Simple French Food* and the *French Menu Cookbook* that also greatly influenced the woman who would later hire Tower at Chez Panisse, Alice Waters.

"Each course must provide a happy contrast to the one preceding it," Olney wrote, describing his theory on how a menu should proceed.

"At the same time the movement through the various courses should be an ascending one from light, delicate and more complex flavors through progressively richer, more full-bodied and simple favors."

Tower took these words to heart, never forgetting the theatrical elements of a meal and how, in his words, it should resemble "a 3-act play orchestrated around food."

6. A MENU CAN TAKE YOU PLACES YOU'VE NEVER BEEN BEFORE.

After migrating from the East to Northern California, Tower saw a classified ad in the *San Francisco Chronicle*. It read, "Immediate opening in a small innovative French provincial restaurant for inspired energetic chef who will plan and cook menus weekly for a single entrée five-course dinner a la Elizabeth David and Fernand Point. Send resume and sample menus to Chez Panisse."

The restaurant that would become the birthplace of California cuisine—described by Ruth Reichl as "a brand of cooking that is instantly recognizable. It is understated and depends on local ingredients, unusual flavor combinations, and impeccable timing"—was only a year and a half old, its first chef had left, and its proprietor needed help in the kitchen. Tower, who knew Point's work and admired David as much as Olney, thought he was just the right man for the job. He had no resume but felt in good shape as far as the other job require-

ment was concerned. Eighteen of his menus went into the mail for Waters to look at.

Chez Panisse was, and still is, located in a remodeled old Victorian house on Shattuck Avenue in Berkeley. Tower arrived for his first interview around the dinner hour. Guests were in their seats, service was in progress, Waters was cooking—and, Tower was told, too busy to see him. Tower reacted somewhat like Joan Lunden did during that TV demo; he wasn't pleased. As he began to protest his displeasure, loudly, at the door of the kitchen, Waters, with a smile, materialized in front of him, invited him in, pointed to a giant simmering pot full of liquid and said to him, "Do something to that soup."

Tower had never seen a pot that big before. He stuck his finger into it and thought it needed some salt and a little wine and cream. Alice dipped a spoon in and tasted what he had done. "You're hired," she told him.

7. A MENU IS AN EXPRESSION OF PLACE.

After taking over chef's duties, Tower began, over time, to bring his own unique flair to Waters's core philosophy of using the best and freshest ingredients, acquired from local farmers, all prepared and cooked "simply, engaging all your senses" (Waters). There is an old French saying, "*C'est la sauce qui fait la poisson."* (It is the sauce that makes the fish.) While deeply inspired and moved by French culinary tradition, Waters, Tower, and their team went a different way. They believed that the fish is the thing and while the sauce can highlight a flavor, a dish's success depends on the freshness of the main ingredients and the skill of the chef in letting the essence of those ingredients find their full expression on the plate.

Chez Panisse attracted first local, then national and international attention. As he grew in confidence, Tower engineered a series of

theme dinners that paid homage to various regions of France—Brittany, Provence, Champagne. After these came tributes to Escoffier, Elizabeth David, Richard Olney, and a special Alice B. Toklas dinner on the one hundredth anniversary of the birth of Gertrude Stein (who grew up in neighboring Oakland). From there they went further afield, with evenings dedicated to the cuisines of Morocco-Tunisia and Corsica.

But the irony of all this was not lost on Tower or Waters. Here they were, people who espoused the virtues of the local and the fresh, and yet they had never done a tribute dinner to their own locality. And so Tower sat down and composed a menu that represented, in his mind, "a celebration of our new sense of place, of where we lived and ate." This turned out to be one of his last dinners at Chez Panisse. He would leave the next year and then come back for a short stint before finally going off to create his own celebrations at Stars. Here is that regional menu, as it appeared to the lucky souls who were there that evening.

The Northern California Regional Dinner
October 7, 1976
Spenger's Tomales Bay bluepoint oysters on ice
Cream of fresh corn soup, Mendocino style, with crayfish butter
Big Sur Garraputa Creek smoked trout steamed
over California bay leaves
Monterey Bay prawns sautéed with garlic, parsley, and butter
Preserved California geese from Sebastopol
Vela dry Monterey Jack cheese from Sonoma
Fresh caramelized figs
Walnuts, almonds, and mountain pears from the
San Francisco Farmers' Market

WHAT TO NAME YOUR DAUGHTER: ALICE, OF COURSE

For foodie couples who are about to have a baby girl, there can be only one choice for a name, Alice, based on its grand lineage in the world of food.

Alice Waters.

Alice B. Toklas.

Alice Trillin, the wife of Calvin, the humorist and food writer who often referred to his wife in his writing and even mentioned her in the title of one of his books.

Alice Brock of Stockbridge, Massachusetts. She's the Alice of "Alice's Restaurant," although there was no restaurant by that name, at least not when Arlo Guthrie wrote and performed the song. It's a complicated story, but Arlo will unwind it for you in his funny first-person account relating how you can get anything you want at Alice's Restaurant—"exceptin' Alice."

Alice of *Alice Doesn't Live Here Anymore*, the Marty Scorsese film about a country-singing woman who works as a waitress at a truck stop diner; the movie later became the basis for a popular television series, also set in a diner and naturally named Alice.

Alice Liddell, the real-life inspiration for Lewis Carroll's fictional Alice, who saw lobsters dance, heard a mock turtle sing about soup ("Beautiful soup, so rich and green, waiting in a hot tureen"), testified in a trial about the theft of the Queen's tarts, and participated in other foodie adventures.

As for what to name a boy, it's more of a muddle. Daniel has some foodie cred: Dan Barber, Blue Hill and Daniel Boulud, Daniel. So does César: César Ramirez, Chef's Table at Brooklyn Fare; César Ritz, the luxury hotelier of long ago; and César, a character in a series of vintage French films that inspired the young Alice Waters. We'll keep investigating.

THOSE WHO ARE PURISTS AND THOSE WHO ARE NOT

ALICE WATERS GOES TO WASHINGTON AND EXPOSES THE RIFTS IN THE FOOD WORLD

People's reputations go in and out of favor, just like their tastes in food. So it is with Alice Waters, "the dowager queen of the grown-locally movement" (as writer Caitlin Flanagan, not a fan, described her). Her standing in the food world came under assault when she penned an open letter to Barack Obama just before his inauguration to his first term in January 2009.

Her letter sought to influence, and ultimately change, the government's policies on food. Becoming public as it did in the days before a new president was taking office, it set off a controversy that resonates to this day, in part because it exposed two major foodie camps: Those Who Are Purists and Those Who Are Not. Although the two camps share many of the same characteristics, the nonpurists have

definite issues with the purists, and all this broke dramatically into the open with the Waters's letter.

THOSE WHO ARE PURISTS SEE THEMSELVES AS REVOLUTIONARIES.

Published online by *Gourmet*, the letter is a manifesto of Purist doctrine. After congratulating Obama on his victory, Waters asks him to join "in a grassroots food revolution that I believe will make a tremendous difference to the health, security, and values of all Americans." Throughout her career, revolution has been an oft-repeated theme of hers. "My delicious revolution began when, young and naïve, I started a restaurant and went looking for good tasting food to cook," she has written.

Her justifiably acclaimed restaurant, Chez Panisse, is in Berkeley. Berkeley is of course the home of the University of California campus that served as a center of protest during the Vietnam War and remains a Left Coast bastion of progressive politics. Waters grew up in that era, identifies with it, and the language of the letter—"Local, affordable, nutritious food should be a right for everyone and not just a privilege for a few"—seems a deliberate echo of those fiery revolutionary days of yore.

But Daniel Patterson, an admirer of Waters who is the former chef of San Francisco's Coi restaurant, wishes she'd chill a little on the Paris Commune rhetoric, arguing that it's "a kind of lightning rod for Berkeley liberal elitism. There's a tone of certainty, of almost religious fervor, that puts a lot of people off. It's unfortunate because the core of her message is important."

THOSE WHO ARE PURISTS ARE ELITISTS.

Ironically, given her populist feelings and language, Waters's critics see her more as a 1-percenter who is out of touch with the way most

Americans live, and how much they can spend on food. In a scathing attack on her, Carla Spartos of the *New York Post* denounced Waters as a "gourmonster" and a member of "the food police"—another food cop, in her view, is fellow Berkeleyite Michael Pollan—both of whom "are on a crusade to tell you not just what you should eat, but how you should eat it."

"Leading the culinary cops is Alice Waters, the poster child of all things local, organic and sustainable," Spartos wrote. "But her actual cooking, which mainly centers around painstakingly composed salads, has always been overshadowed by her cooking philosophy: a chiding and bourgeois brand of junk food prohibitionism."

Exhibit A against Waters, according to Spartos, was a *60 Minutes* interview she did with Leslie Stahl during this time in which she revealed how she paid ten dollars for a bag of green market grapes. When Stahl inquired about this, Waters responded defensively, "And some people want to buy Nike shoes—two pairs."

"One might wonder to whom she is referring," says Spartos.

SNOB ADVICE

Whatever your view of Waters on this issue, her basic rules of eating and cooking—as outlined in her book *The Art of Simple Food*—are worth keeping in mind: "1. Eat locally and sustainably. 2. Eat seasonally. 3. Shop at farmers' markets. 4. Plant a garden. 5. Conserve, compost, recycle. 6. Cook simply, engaging all your senses. 7. Cook together. 8. Eat together. 9. Remember food is precious."

THOSE WHO ARE PURISTS ADMIT THEY'RE PURISTS, BUT THEY SAY THEY HAVE TO BE TO EFFECT THE CHANGES THEY SEEK.

In the midst of the controversy, Scott Kraft of the *Los Angeles Times* went to the barricades for Waters, writing a flattering piece entitled "She yanks their food chains." The chains she was yanking belonged to those who compromised on food, unlike Waters who, said Kraft, "doesn't compromise."

This no-compromise philosophy is a point of virtue among Waters and her supporters, because as they see it, the stakes involved—reforming agribusiness, promoting organic farming and ranching, getting more people to eat healthier, improving school nutrition, ending hunger, fighting obesity and diseases linked to poor diet—are so high.

"She's an absolutist, which is a great strength," said her friend, Michael Pollan. "She's staking out a pure position, and every movement needs that." The author of *The Omnivore's Dilemma* issued his own letter to the president, calling for "reform of the entire food system."

While there is sympathy and perhaps even broad agreement with many of the goals of Those Who Are Purists, James Thurber, a professor at the American University in Washington DC and an expert on government lobbying, would like to see more details. "They don't have a central core message," he told *the Washington Post*. "Is this about reducing obesity in schools? Is it about pesticides on the farms? It's a wonderful thing to try to change policy, but what policy are they trying to change?"

THOSE WHO ARE PURISTS ARE HOLIER THAN THOU.

"It's a moral issue for me," Waters has said, referring to her push for organic food. "Everyone on this planet deserves to eat food that's

really nourishing and produced in a way that is fair to the people who produce it."

No one doubts the depth of her passion or the sincerity of her beliefs, yet her moral certitude is but one more reason why Those Who Are Purists tick people off, including—you know he'd get into this scrap eventually, right?—Anthony Bourdain.

"I'll tell you," he told an interviewer when all this was trending everywhere. "Alice Waters annoys the living sh*t out of me. We're all in the middle of a recession, like we're all going to start buying expensive organic food and running to the green market. There's something very Khmer Rouge about Alice Waters that has become unrealistic. I mean I'm not crazy about our obsession with corn or ethanol and all that, but I'm a little uncomfortable with legislating good eating habits. I'm suspicious of orthodoxy, the kind of orthodoxy when it comes to what you put in your mouth."

Bourdain later did some serious backfill on these remarks, backing off on the Khmer Rouge comment and complimenting Waters as a "visionary whose accomplishments clearly dwarf my own." He added encomiums about her "enormous contribution to changing the way we eat and cook today" and that Chez Panisse was "inarguably a cradle of the food revolution," all unassailable points.

Nevertheless, after Bourdain entered the scrum, Frank Bruni of the *New York Times* piled on too, criticizing Bourdain for being out of line (not the first time) but also Waters for "her fantasy" that cash-strapped American families would and should start buying ten-dollar bags of grapes. "There's some class-inflected hypocrisy in the food world," wrote Bruni, looking at the big picture, "where the center seems to be ceding territory to two wings: the self-appointed sophis-

ticates and the supposed rubes." Bruni, Bourdain, and Waters belong to the first category, but clearly they like to fight with each other too.

THOSE WHO ARE PURISTS ARE HYPOCRITES.

Coinciding with the release of the letter, Waters and other food activists organized a series of pre-inaugural dinners at private homes around Washington, DC. The guest list consisted of the powerful, the wealthy, and the connected, and brand-name chefs such as Daniel Boulud, Rick Bayless, and Tom Colichio did the cooking. The exclusive guest list and the cost per meal—five hundred dollars per plate—drew more charges of elitism, charges rejected by the organizers. "Good food is not for snooty elitists," responded Ayelet Waldman, a Berkeley novelist who helped put on the dinners. "It's an issue for everybody."

The dinners raised one hundred thousand dollars for local food charities, and yet the criticism did not stop. Daniel Maurer of Grub Street pointed out the apparent contradiction of the locavore Waters hosting an event in which a dozen celebrity chefs and their teams flew in to Washington from around the country. Many of them also brought food with them, and there were reports of fresh California produce, fish, and other items being imported just for the occasion.

"Here's a heads up for the future, Dan Barber," said Maurer to the prominent New York chef and farm-to-table guru who also helmed a DC dinner that week. "It's not local or seasonal if you have to put it on a plane."

THOSE WHO ARE PURISTS ARE STIFLING CREATIVITY WITH THEIR ORTHODOXIES.

Waters called for the replacement of White House chef Cristeta Comerford, a protégée of the previous White House chef, Walter Scheib, who took umbrage at her remarks. He said that Comerford

had done a fine job for the Bushes and would do the same for the Obamas and that she was being treated "like so many pounds of chopped liver." He added that he was speaking out because Comerford—who ultimately kept her job—could not publicly defend herself due to the political sensitivity of her post.

Scheib's remarks brought applause from Washington restaurant critic Todd Kliman, who repeated the familiar criticisms of Waters as being overly righteous and inflexible. Yet he also introduced an interesting new angle to the debate—the idea that "local" and "seasonal" may be outmoded concepts due to another trending concept, that of globalization.

"What Waters espoused was really just an –ism," Kliman wrote. "A good –ism, a necessary –ism, but an –ism all the same. And –isms have their limitations. Why, for instance, should top-flight chefs content themselves with using only what's local and seasonal when the emergence of new technologies has made it easier than ever to bring in delicacies around the globe? Yet many do. I've even seen some chefs so desperate to be perceived as gastronomically correct that they have lied about their purveyors on their menus."

QUOTABLE SNOB

More from Todd Kliman: "At the moment [2009], the best, most exciting food in the world is to be found in Spain. Yes, the country is blessed with an abundance of good natural resources. But its chefs look around the world for inspiration and are more inclined to want to manipulate and enhance flavors than to present them simply. And why not? Cooking, after all, is not about doing good; it's about tasting good."

THOSE WHO ARE PURISTS HAVE A MISGUIDED EMPHASIS THAT IS HURTING THE VERY PEOPLE THEY SEEK TO HELP.

One full year after her letter and the pre-inaugural dinners, the *Atlantic* published a piece that tore into Waters anew, with Caitlin Flanagan ripping her efforts to teach gardening and good nutrition to schoolchildren, particularly the poor and underprivileged. Flanagan argued that the Edible Schoolyard project was a "cruel trick" that deprived Hispanic students of the time they need to study English and math, which will truly improve their lives and boost their career earning potential, as opposed to digging around in the dirt in service to a back-to-the-land ideology favored by privileged urbanites.

Flanagan quoted a favorite maxim of Waters—"Gardens help students to learn the pleasure of physical work"—and then stuck in the knife. "Does the immigrant farm worker dream that his child will learn to enjoy manual labor, or that his child will be freed from it? What is the goal of an education, of what we once called 'book learning'? These are questions best left unasked when it comes to the gardens."

Flanagan has nothing against teaching kids about gardens; she just thinks it should be done after school, like the way sports or chorus or chess club are handled. But it damages a child's education when it becomes part of the school curriculum, she argues.

As might be expected, the Flanagan piece generated considerable backlash among Waters's many supporters, including Ed Levine of Serious Eats. He did a point-by-point deconstruction of it in his blog, saying that it was not an either/or proposition, that a child could learn English and math as well as gardening and that one did not preclude the other. He called the piece "a hatchet job," "character assassination," "wrongheaded," "belligerent, "fueled by an animus," "ridiculously far-fetched," "poorly reasoned mud slinging," and "inflammatory bullsh*t."

Inflammatory bullsh*t? Poorly reasoned mud slinging? Character assassination? Now we're talking about the world of food we've come to know and love!

HOW SHRIMP ~~WENBERG~~ NEWBURG CAME TO BE

Having started the chapter with Pierre Franey, it seems only right to end it with him. In his first book he tells the story of how Shrimp Newburg got its name. It's a story that Franey heard when he first came to this country in the years before World War II.

In the late 1800s a man named Wenberg dined frequently at Delmonico's in Manhattan, an elite establishment renowned for its steak. But Wenberg's favorite meal was a creation of his own, a rich shrimp dish made with cream, egg yolks, and sherry. He handed the recipe over to the kitchen and ate it so often that the staff named it after him. Shrimp Wenberg became an item on the menu and the favorite of other diners too.

Then a bitter fight erupted between Wenberg and the owner of Delmonico's, who, in a fit of pique, purged his name from the menu and depriving his antagonist of his one shot at immortality, renamed the dish Shrimp Newburg. So it is known today. Remember this story if you ever hear anyone suggest that fighting about food is somehow a new thing.

Addendum: In 1939, when Pierre Franey came here, the avocado was basically unknown in France, and the first one he ever saw was at the New York World's Fair. People called it an avocado then and still do today.

FOODIE SNOB QUIZ #3
THE PRESIDENTIAL PALATE

Like Mr. Smith before her, Alice Waters idealistically went to Washington to change how things are done and stir things up. Although she did not achieve all she had hoped, she brought attention to the traditional role of the president as a national leader in affairs of food, dining, and entertaining.

This quiz tests your knowledge of American presidents and how they ate, drank, and entertained. Don't peek at the answers that follow the quiz.

1. This president, whose family has a history of public service, had a profound dislike of broccoli. He refused to eat it while in the White House, displeasing farmers who grew the vegetable. His name, please.

   a. Teddy Roosevelt

   b. Franklin Roosevelt

   c. John Quincy Adams

   d. George H. W. Bush

2. Cristeta Comerford was the first female to serve as White House chef. She did so under two presidents (George W. Bush and Barack Obama) and is an American immigrant born in another country. Where was her birthplace?

   a. Ireland

   b. Brazil

   c. Philippines

   d. South Africa

3. While on the campaign trail, Bill Clinton loved to eat pizza. But back at the White House they would not let him order it. Why not?

   a. When in the White House, presidents are not permitted to eat any food that is not prepared and cooked there.

   b. He was kept on a stricter diet, due to concerns about his health and weight.

   c. The Secret Service must first taste any food brought into the president from outside the White House, and Clinton rejected this practice.

   d. The White House does not accept food deliveries such as pizza for security reasons.

4. Despite his patrician bearing and background, Franklin Delano Roosevelt liked nonpatrician fare such as fish chowder, grilled cheese sandwiches, and hot dogs. According to White House housekeeper Henrietta Nesbitt, what was his unlikely favorite dessert?

   a. fruitcake

   b. Lindy's cheesecake from New York, his home state

   c. root beer float

   d. Texas peach cobbler, a home-state favorite of his vice president, John Nance Garner

5. Concerns about food industry practices are hardly new. Upton Sinclair's investigative novel, *The Jungle*, exposed the unclean conditions and harsh animal cruelty practices in Chicago's meatpacking industry. Responding to the national outrage, this rough-riding president met with Sinclair at the White House and introduced a bill to clean up the industry.

    a. Jimmy Carter

    b. Ulysses S. Grant

    c. Harry Truman

    d. Teddy Roosevelt

6. Dolley Madison, wife of the fourth American president, James Madison, was called "America's first First Lady" because she turned the White House into an exciting social setting for dinners and entertaining. Although Thomas Jefferson had a recipe for it and George and Martha Washington served it at Mount Vernon, she receives credit for popularizing this dessert.

    a. key lime pie

    b. ice cream

    c. chocolate chip cookies

    d. cherry pie

7. Ronald Reagan had a sweet tooth too. He loved a certain kind of candy and snacked on it during cabinet meetings, as did everyone else in the meeting who wished to court favor with him. What was the candy?

    a. M&Ms

    b. Skittles

    c. jellybeans

    d. Jolly Ranchers

8. During the Reagan era, Princess Diana and her droopy husband dined on lobster mousseline with Maryland crab at the White House. After dinner, by special arrangement, she danced with a dashing Hollywood leading man who was also in attendance. Lady Di had developed a youthful crush on him after seeing him dance in the movies. Who was the star?

a. Harrison Ford

b. Fred Astaire

c. John Travolta

d. Patrick Swayze

9. President Donald Trump owns luxury properties around the world, including the Trump Hotel on Central Park West in Manhattan. Name the Michelin three-star chef whose eponymous restaurant is on the first floor of this hotel.(Trivia: One of his restaurants is said to have invented chocolate molten cake, a fad of a while back.)

a. Masa Takayama

b. Daniel Humm

c. Joël Robuchon

d. Jean-Georges Vongerichten

10. Which American president, known for his love of good food, wine, and the joys of the land, made this statement: "I have often thought that if heaven had given me choice of my position, it should have been a rich spot on earth, well watered. No occupation is so delightful to me as the culture of the earth, and no culture comparable to that of a garden."

a. George Washington

b. Thomas Jefferson

c. Abraham Lincoln

d. Teddy Roosevelt

Answers: 1. d; 2. c; 3. a; 4. a; 5. d; 6. b; 7. c; 8. c; 9. d; 10. b

CHAPTER FOUR

Cooking, and other acts of self-invention

In this chapter we talk about the pleasures of cooking at home, and the discoveries that can arise from it. "Part of what we do as cooks," said the pastry chef Gina DePalma, "is to get people to open their minds and then palates to new things." A kitchen is an enormously creative place. It is where you make the meals that nourish yourself and your family, but it is also where you discover new things that lead you into worlds far beyond your home. If the previous chapter extolled a few of the names of French cuisine, here we turn homeward again, to some American stars of the kitchen.

A THING FOR SALAD

THE STORY OF NEWMAN'S OWN

In the summer of 1956, a show business columnist interviewed the young Paul Newman before the premiere of *Somebody Up There Likes Me,* Newman's breakout role as a movie actor. His portrayal of the hard-luck boxer Rocky Graziano—a role originally slotted for James Dean, before his fatal car crash—turned him from an unknown into a major Hollywood star.

It's not clear if the columnist, Sidney Skolsky, went to lunch with Newman or found out about his eating habits just by talking to him, but they made an impression on him. "He is an enthusiastic chef," he wrote. "He is proud of his 'Newman Celery Salad.' Dining out, he is likely to prepare the salad himself."

On one of Newman's first dates with Joanne Woodward, at Chasen's in Beverly Hills, they brought a salad to the table that was too oily for him. Politely excusing himself, he stood up, took his plate into the bathroom, washed the lettuce, dried it with towels, then came back to the table and dressed the greens lightly with oil and a little water. Pronouncing himself satisfied, he resumed his meal and their conversation.

This would not be the last time he would do this in their dating and marriage. Newman had a thing for salad the way some people insist on their fries coming out hot, not lukewarm or, God forbid, cold, and if

they do not receive their fries in this manner they instantly send them back to the kitchen and demand more. Newman was the same way about his salad, except that rather than leave it to the kitchen to fix the problem, he'd do it himself, asking the waiter to bring fresh greens to the table, undressed, so he could prepare them the way he liked. Even after he became famous he did this—the others at the restaurant, the waiters, star-struck patrons, and his understanding wife, looking on with a mixture of admiration, puzzlement, and amusement.

Newman's thing for salad began when he was young and continued well after his blue-eyed charm and matinee-idol good looks—not to mention movies such as *Hud*, *Cool Hand Luke*, *Butch Cassidy and the Sundance Kid*, *The Sting*, and *Cars* (his last; he voiced Doc Hudson)—made him one of the most admired men in America. Nor was he particular about it only when he went out; he wanted his dressing to be just right back home in Westport, Connecticut, too. Unhappy with most bottled dressings, he started doing what home chefs do everywhere: fiddling around with the recipe to get the taste exactly the way he liked. When his children came home from college or wherever they were, they left again with his homemade salad dressing, packaged up for them in converted wine bottles.

QUOTABLE SNOB

Asked once about his various charitable and philanthropic activities, Paul Newman said, "I'm not running for sainthood. I just happen to think that in life we need to be a little like the farmer, who puts back into the soil what he takes out."

It was a tradition when the children were young for the family to go Christmas caroling around the neighborhood. Then one year Newman decided to hand out bottles of his dressing to his neighbors as gifts. But in order to do this, he needed to produce much larger quantities than usual. So he recruited his best buddy, the writer A. E. Hotchner, who also lived in town, to help him. The two of them retreated into an old barn on Newman's fifteen-acre farmhouse property and fell to mixing giant batches of olive oil, vinegar, and seasonings, per the recipe, after which they bottled it all up.

The giveaway was a smash hit, the salad dressing equivalent of *Somebody Up There Likes Me*. People really did seem to like it too, and not just because of who the recipe maker was. Thus inspired, Newman and Hotchner decided to turn their little lark into a business—not a serious one, mind you, just something on the side, something they could have a little fun with and that maybe they could sell at Stew Leonard's, an organic food shop and dairy in the area. Newman had once thought about starting his own restaurant in town, an idea that never came to pass. But he had always liked the name he was going to use, so they put it to work instead for his new business: Newman's Own.

One thing he would not permit, however, is his photograph on the front label. That was just too much. Newman agreed, however, to an illustration of himself, as long as it was done in a humorous way. Adding to the merriment was Hotchner, a witty playwright and author—for an entertaining read, pick up his *The Man Who Lived at the Ritz*, his Casablanca-like historical novel with details about the Hotel Ritz, Lipp's Bistro, Maxim's, and other aspects of German-occupied Paris during WWII—who chipped in with some clever advertising slogans:

"The Star of Oil and Vinegar and the Oil and Vinegar of the Stars"

"Fine Foods Since February"

And, after they produced a pasta sauce: "The Intimate Companion Your Pasta Will Never Forget"

Though his friend has passed on, the nonagenarian Hotchner continues to write. He also raises chickens at his home in Westport and has a menagerie of peacocks and a pet African parrot, "Ernie," which he named after Ernest Hemingway, a one-time drinking buddy of his. Evidently though, it is hard to accurately assess a parrot's gender, so Hotchner hired a Stamford company to do a DNA test on the bird. Turns out Ernie is a girl, "except now," as he relates, "it is short for Ernestine." In the morning he takes off the top of the cage and Ernestine asks him how he is doing, in French.

The official debut of Newman's Own salad dressing occurred in August 1982.

It appeared on the shelf at Stew Leonard's for $1.19 a bottle, selling out quickly, and the two mainly-in-it-for-a-laugh owners might have settled for that, except that it jumped off store shelves everywhere, all across the country. Suddenly they had a business—a real business. "We never had a plan," said Newman. "Hotch and I comprise two of the great witless people in business. We are a testament to the theory of Random, whatever that means."

What it meant was sales. Newman's Own earned more than five hundred thousand dollars in six months—sixty-five thousand dollars of it targeted to charity, mainly to the nonprofit foundation that had been set up in the memory of Newman's son who had died of a drug and alcohol overdose four years earlier. One minor glitch in the early days came when an influential food critic—ah, those critics!—derided the salad dressing as being too oily. That struck a nerve with Newman, who ordered a refashioning of the formula to make it a dressing that absolutely no one, ever, would take to the bathroom and wash off. Customers seemed to like the change, and Newman's Own went on to produce its own brand of pasta sauce, lemonade, popcorn, cookies, and other products, including an organic line.

One of the company's missions is to donate all its profits to charity. At the time of Newman's death, in 2008, at age eighty-three, Newman's Own had donated more than two hundred million dollars to charitable and nonprofit organizations.

4 INDISPUTABLE THINGS ABOUT MARTHA STEWART

ALTHOUGH SOME, NO DOUBT, WILL DISPUTE THIS

It is typically not good style to start a story with an addendum. Nevertheless, here it is: After the success of their Christmas giveaway, Newman and Hotchner decided to hold a blind tasting of their salad oil to see how it fared against other commercial dressings on the market. To organize the tasting, they turned to another Westport resident who was just beginning to gain notice as a cook, party planner, and arbiter of style. Her name: Martha Stewart.

Things worked out fairly well for Martha after that (for the most part), although she is, and always will be, a person about whom other persons, particularly of the female gender, have strong, keenly felt opinions, pro and con.

We do believe, however, there are four indisputable statements about Martha that all food people, and people in general, can agree on. Perhaps. Maybe. Well, probably not. But we'll try anyway.

1. MARTHA IS IN THE MIDST OF A RENAISSANCE.

Proof of this is that the millennials generally like her and admire her. She's like a grandmother figure to them; they are only vaguely aware, if at all, of the hostilities of the past, and mostly don't care about them anyway. While planning the opening of his new Napa Valley restaurant, Charter Oak, the Michelin three-star chef Christopher Kostow told a reporter that he envisioned the place as "Martha Stewart's dream." Across the country in Brooklyn, Luis Ilades of the hipsterish Urban Rustic market and cafe said that Martha used to be "someone your mother would follow." But now, having served time, she has real street cred. "She's such a Suzy Homemaker and also did some time in the joint," he said admiringly.

Stewart's website is one of the top-pinned sites on Pinterest, ahead of its rivals in the crafts-homemaking-cooking sphere where she competes. Martha, notes reporter Christine Haughney, "has emerged as something of a patron saint for entrepreneurial hipsters, 20- and 30-somethings who have begun their own pickling, cupcake and letterpress businesses and are selling crafty goods online."

In Jen Lancaster's book, *The Tao of Martha*, she spends a year trying to do things the way Martha would, if Martha were in her shoes. Lancaster admires how her idol does not keep her knowledge selfishly to herself but rather shares it with others. Writer Hillary Kelly agrees, saying she "embraced homegrown DIY culture long before it invaded the mainstream. Martha isn't influencing hipster culture; she created it."

2. MARTHA CAN BE A LITTLE, AHEM, PRICKLY AT TIMES.

Despite her status as a role model for hipsters and millennials, Martha does not exactly coddle them. She disapproves of tattoos and recommends embroidering a jacket or a silk screen T-shirt if you would like to make a colorful personal statement. And in remarks to a British luxury publication, she went off on younger generations for what she sees as a lack of initiative. "I think every business is trying to target millennials," she said. "Now we are finding out that they are living with their parents. They don't have the initiative to go out and find a little apartment and grow a tomato plant on the terrace."

While sympathizing with the challenging economic conditions that some young people face, you still "have to work for it. You have to strive for it. You have to go after it," she continued. "I got married at 19 and I immediately got an apartment and I fixed it up. I was very proud of everything I did. I got the furniture at auctions for pennies. Beautiful furniture. My apartments were lovely and homey and comfortable."

3. MARTHA IS A SYMBOL, ALTHOUGH WHAT SHE SYMBOLIZES DEPENDS ON WHO YOU ARE.

A stockbroker in her younger days, Stewart spent five months in a West Virginia prison and five more months in home detention after being convicted of lying to authorities during an insider-trading investigation early in the 2000s. Some have argued that authorities unfairly targeted her because she is such a high-profile figure. In any event she remains a target of ridicule and criticism for this and other reasons.

Hillary Kelly's term for it is *Marthafreude*, people who just love to hate her and see her fail. She is, in the words of one inflicted with this

condition, "the domestic goddess who can supposedly cook, decorate and even get herself into and out of jail." Another called her "a control freakish middle brow taste maker."

The novelist Ruth Pennebaker admitted, "I don't hate many people, but I do hate Martha Stewart." She confessed she had an uncomfortable feeling that her life as a mother and career woman was vastly inferior to Stewart's. Whereas she spent her days "writing and getting rejected and driving carpools and battling our little roach infestation problem and wondering whether I should put a bag over my head," the beautiful blonde Stewart always had it together. "She was always whipping up something tasty and nutritious and attractive and she never lost her megawatt smile or her ex-model's posture or her steely discipline."

Perfect is a word associated with Martha. It is a concept she strives for and is, in her mind, relatively easy to achieve, that is, if one follows her advice. There is one way to do things, her way, and if you would like your dinner party or home decor to be perfect, you have no choice but to do them that way. Otherwise you run the risk of being hopelessly and terminally gauche.

This fixation on perfection is without a doubt the one thing that drives her critics—and some of her fans—crazy. One magazine writer mocked her as "perfectly perfect" and imagined that "on a typical morning she's already fed the chickens, built a toolshed and launched a new business by the time the rest of us are stumbling in the shower." Another derided her as "perfect Martha, with her Armani suits and her three sizes of loppers." Her daughter Alexis, who probably knows her mother better than anyone else, can't stand this side of her. "If I didn't do something perfectly, I had to do it again," she said. "I grew up with a glue gun pointed at my head."

"She just needs to be quiet. She's a movie star. If she were confident in her acting, she wouldn't be trying to be Martha Stewart."

—MARTHA STEWART ON GWYNETH PALTROW,
who has developed a second career as a cookbook
author and lifestyle consultant a la Martha

4. MORE WOMEN THAN MEN HAVE ISSUES WITH MARTHA.

All the critics quoted in this piece are women, and virtually all the critics we found in our research for this piece were women. That is not to say that men do not have problems with her—surely they do—but it is not unreasonable to suggest that women take their issues with Martha much more *personally* than men.

In her Martha analysis, Ruth Pennebaker went all the way back to her teen years, fantasizing about what Martha would have done if she had gone to Pennebaker's high school. "Martha was the cheerleader, the pep squad leader, the class president, the style avatar, the girl whose hair flipped perfectly and whose calendar bulged with dates and activities," wrote Pennebaker, who resented Martha even though Martha may or may not have done any of these things as a girl.

Stewart, born Martha Kostyra, grew up in a Polish-American family in Nutley, New Jersey. The Kostyras attended Our Lady of Mount Carmel Church, and the parish priest came over to their house at Easter to have dinner and bless the food. She learned to cook from her mom, who made cabbage pierogis, Sauerbraten, beef tongue, and *galumpkis*, Polish cabbage rolls. Martha's philosophy as expressed in her senior class statement in the Nutley High yearbook—"I do what I please, and I do it with ease"—carried her through a Barnard education; marriage; the birth of Alexis; divorce; a pioneering career as

Although she no longer lives there, Martha's name will be forever linked to Turkey Hill, the Westport, Connecticut, farmhouse estate where she once arranged tasting parties for Paul Newman and filmed episodes of her television series.

It derives its name from its address, 48 Turkey Hill Road South, and Martha lived in the restored 1805 farmhouse with her then-husband and daughter for three decades. It was her countrified DIY take on Breakers or Hearst Castle. She planted trees, an orchard, and vegetable gardens; built a pergola and brick terrace; raised chickens; bought a dissembled 1900 Connecticut tobacco barn and had it reassembled on the property; furnished the house with period antiques; and built a swimming pool. The concrete pool, said admiring friend Lloyd Allen, was painted black because she envisioned it as "one of those shimmering, depthless rectangles you see in the front of a museum."

Before the Stewarts came to Turkey Hill, *New Yorker* writer John Hersey lived there. The house served as a television studio, and it was where she conducted her business affairs when not in Manhattan, about an hour's drive away. It was also where she interviewed Audrey

Doneger, who was applying to be a cook for her catering company in the early 1980s when Martha was just starting out. Doneger made some cookies for her first job interview. Martha liked them, hired her, and then assigned her to make a huge batch of them for a party she was organizing the next day.

Doneger worked frenetically all night to fill the order and met Martha the next morning with the cookies, nervously sitting and waiting as her new boss took a bite of one, in silence. "You don't schmooze with Martha," explains Doneger. "She's not going to have a pajama party with you. She's a different species."

The different species frowned in disapproval. The cookie wasn't nearly as good as yesterday. What happened?

Doneger explained that she had gotten so tired and so behind schedule that rather than make the cookies by hand, as she had done before, she used a Cuisinart. Martha could taste the difference between a Cuisinart cookie and one made by hand. She gave Doneger some money to buy all the butter, sugar, and flour she needed, and told her to go home and learn how to make big batches of cookies. The right way.

a lifestyle expert, author, publisher, television personality, and product developer; business successes and failures; and a career bounce back from time in the joint.

Even so, writer Margaret Talbot sees her as a throwback to the days when a woman's place was strictly in the home. "If Stewart is a throwback, it's not so much to the 1950s as the 1850s." She derides her as a "corporate overachiever turned domestic superachiever" and the head of "a lifestyle cult."

Talbot and others associate Martha with the picture-perfect homemaker she plays on television—but Rebecca Harrington, for one, isn't sure why. She points out that men do not look at George Clooney and think they need to become a rich movie star with a gorgeous attorney-activist wife. "And yet, Martha, by virtue of her very imitability, somehow encourages us to twist ourselves into knots of aspirational inadequacy," she writes in *Salon*. "Why is it that when we see an ideal it immediately and unquestionably invokes a personal comparison?"

Dunno. But we are certain that if Martha is involved, people will fight about it.

HOW TO PUBLISH A COOKBOOK

IRMA ROMBAUER DID IT. SO CAN YOU

Joy of Cooking is a cookbook for the ages—and a publishing story for the ages too. Originally self-published in 1931, it has sold millions of copies; generations of mothers, daughters, fathers, and sons have cooked from it; and home cooks today as well as Michelin-star chefs consider it a foundational work that belongs in every cook's library.

How Irma S. Rombauer—the first and original author, with an assist from daughter Marion—brought *Joy* into print, against all odds, is an inspirational and instructive story. Ever thought of writing a cookbook of your own? Here are six things we can learn from this determined woman's example.

DON'T WORRY ABOUT THE TITLE.
Some authors get hung up on the title before they've even written a word. The title for the first edition of Rombauer's work was *The Joy of Cooking: A Compilation of Reliable Recipes with a Casual Culinary Chat*. Note the *The* at the start—they dropped it in subsequent editions to create the beautifully precise *Joy of Cooking*—and somebody also rewrote that subtitle, thankfully. Concentrate on the work;

make that as strong as you can, and the title and subtitle will take care of themselves.

A PUBLISHER, ALMOST CERTAINLY, WILL NOT BE INTERESTED IN YOUR BOOK.

Here, we are referring to publishers that pay *you* for your work, as opposed to Create Space or other self-publishing entities where you put up the dollars to get your book into print or digital form. It is reassuring to note, though—and this is one reason why Irma's story is so wonderful—that she self-published her book. Few of her friends thought this was a good idea; most thought it a trifle hare-brained. A couple even tried to talk her out of it because it represented such a big risk for her.

Her attorney-husband Edgar, upon his death, had left her an inheritance of six thousand dollars; she spent fully half of it on production for the book and an initial print run of three thousand copies. She did this at the onset of the Depression, when many of her neighbors in St. Louis and millions of others across the country were out of work and struggling to pay the rent or find enough to eat every day. She had no job. She was fifty-four years old and Edgar, who suffered from depression, had just committed suicide. Think you have roadblocks to publishing? Remember Irma.

A PUBLISHER WILL LIKELY NOT BE INTERESTED IN YOUR BOOK EVEN IF IT BECOMES A SELF-PUBLISHING SUCCESS.

Many of the recipes in the first edition came from Irma's friends and neighbors in the German-American section of St. Louis where she lived. This was also a natural constituency of people who agreed to buy the book. She sold to them and in local bookshops and stores as well. But it was her mail order business—selling to people she did not know, who had heard good things about it via word of mouth—

that convinced her she had a hit on her hands. Smartly she released the book ahead of the Christmas gift-giving season, and during this heady time she giddily wrote a friend saying she could almost pinch herself because "so far every day has brought from 10 to 20 orders."

With the book selling so well, it occurred to her that a mainstream publisher might be interested in taking it on and distributing it to a national audience. She queried Simon & Schuster and other New York publishers and received rejection letters from all. A respected St. Louis publisher, Bobbs-Merrill, at least paid her the courtesy of looking at the book and reviewing it in-house. The reader reports were not good. One called it "just another cookbook," another saw it as "awfully tame." A third said that much of the material appeared to be "legitimately filched," conceding that there were "lots of good recipes between its covers." Bobbs-Merrill turned her down like everyone else.

IN THE FACE OF THE INEVITABLE REJECTIONS AND NEGATIVITY, IT'S GOOD TO HAVE A STRONG CORE NETWORK AROUND YOU.

After getting the cold shoulder from publishers, Irma got terribly down and discouraged—an unavoidable part of the writing and publishing process. Fortunately she had a strong core of friends and family to fall back on, the same people who had helped her through the bad times after her husband's death.

One of them was her daughter Marion Rombauer Becker. She had tested recipes during the research and writing phase, proofread the manuscript and performed other editorial tasks, and suggested many of the art and design touches that made the first edition so attractive, especially when placed next to the rather ordinary-looking cookbooks of the time. (Marion's job description of course evolved over time, and as her mother grew older, she took over as author.)

Another soldier for the cause was Mazie Whyte, Edgar's former secretary at his law office. All these recipes, all these pages, had to be typed, by hand, on a manual typewriter. That was Mazie's job, and she did it faithfully. She compiled the index too.

EVEN WITH HELP, THOUGH, IT'S YOUR BABY. IT'S UP TO YOU.

Following the rejections from Bobbs-Merrill and the others, it would have been understandable for Irma to call it quits. After all, her gamble had paid off. She had sold out her three thousand print run and made her money back and then some. By the standards of self-publishing, including self-publishing today, this was a phenomenal success. She could have easily bid adieu to books and moved on with her life, job well done.

But she did not; she kept going, continuing to try to make *Joy* better, despite all the usual nagging author doubts. Irma once described herself as "ill taught, vaguely informed, moderately gifted." Nor did she consider herself a grand literary stylist. "I am conscious—keenly so—of being a second rate writer," she told an editor.

None of this was true, although she may have felt these feelings in her low moments. Energetic, bubbling over with ideas, a person who—as her original subtitle suggested—just loved to chat about food and cooking, she was a far better writer than she admitted, and her ongoing efforts helped lift the public—and publishing—perception of what cookbooks could be. Bobbs-Merrill reconsidered its earlier rejection and released the first trade edition of the work in 1936; more sales followed and the book became a fixture on the best-seller lists in part because it was not a routine kitchen instructional manual but rather an individual expression of voice and vision. One might even say, literature.

Her description of a sauce also summed up her view of her book: "Having made it good, a great deal has been accomplished, but not enough, it must also look good." As pleasing as it appeared, though, it would never have succeeded as it did without the funny, interesting, informed, delightful, and chatty comments of the woman behind the words. Many things would change about the book over the years, but this was not one of them. *Joy of Cooking* was not a dry tutorial; it was exactly as advertised: a book about the joy of cooking.

SNOB ASIDE

One of the things that distinguished *Joy*—and distinguishes it still—is Irma Rombauer's sense of humor. For the first edition, after finding an old cookbook with a recipe for cooking pigs' feet, she could not help but poke fun at the way it was written: "Pig's Feet. Take your feet, wash them, scratch them, put them on the griddle, cook them to a turn and serve them." Yum!

IRMA'S PUBLISHING STORY ENDS HAPPILY, AND WHO KNOWS? MAYBE YOURS WILL TOO.

Realistically, achieving what Irma Rombauer did—writing and publishing an innovative, best-selling classic that launched a family cookbook enterprise that flourishes to this day—may be beyond your reach. But you never know. Crazier things have happened. One last piece of advice. Confronted as she often was by skeptics who questioned how she could dare to write a book, when she had never done such a thing before, she said merrily, "Oh, do you know, I am a reader!"

This is one of the keys to good writing often forgotten by neophyte writers, including cookery writers. Yes, taste, taste, taste. But also: read, read, read. The tastiest writers do both.

TAKE THAT, FRANCOPHILES!

5 ALL-AMERICAN COOKS AND FOODIES YOU ABSOLUTELY MUST KNOW FOR YOUR NEXT DINNER PARTY

In the last chapter we provided a brief but illuminating guide to all those who wish to name-drop famous French foodies at a dinner party.

Consider this equal time. Here are five wondrous women cooks, Americans all, who have greatly enhanced the national cuisine. Some domestic foodies may know more about foreign cuisines than they do about their own country. Dazzle them with these stories.

EDNA LEWIS

All her life Edna Lewis sought through her cooking to recapture the tastes and flavors of her childhood. Born in 1916, she grew up in Freetown, Virginia, which was founded by her grandfather and other emancipated slaves after the Civil War. Her parents taught at the Freetown school, and Edna's mother made lunches for the students, her daughter watching and assisting at her side. "I learned about cooking and flavor as a child, watching my mother prepare food in our kitchen in Virginia," she recalled. "I suppose I just naturally followed her example."

After her mother and father died, she left Freetown as a teenager and eventually settled in New York City, where she worked odd jobs until her talents as a refined Southern cook became recognized. Beautiful people from the society columns, movies, and the arts—including Tennessee Williams, Truman Capote, and William Faulkner, three Southerners who knew what good cooking tasted like back home—came to eat at Café Nicholson on the Upper East Side, where she ran the kitchen. Being in publishing's capital city, it was inevitable that an editor would approach her about a project, and her cookbooks *The Taste of Country Cooking* and *In Pursuit of Flavor* helped spread the word nationally about her and her style of cuisine.

One thing she found when she first came to New York was that the food didn't taste nearly as good as it did back on the farm. "So it has been my lifelong effort to try and recapture those good flavors of the past," she said. In the summers at Freetown they ate fresh-picked tomatoes and boiled corn on the cob for lunch, and at dinner they had corn again, serving it as a separate course after the main meal had been eaten. In the late fall they'd make beef barley stew after butchering a steer. The steer was hung in the hide, and they carved meat from it as needed. Pretty much the only fish she ever ate as a girl was caught that day at a nearby stream.

SNOB ADVICE

Ideally Lewis cooked corn on the cob the same day it was picked, although if that wasn't possible, she stored the ear in a pot of water to keep it from drying out. She always boiled the corn in the husk because she felt it added flavor and kept in the moisture. Pull back the husk to the bottom of the cob without detaching it, take off the silk strands, and replace the husk over the corn again and tie it closed. Then it's ready for boiling.

Lewis lived long enough—she died in 2006, on the eve of her nineti-eth birthday—to win widespread admiration for her contributions to American cookery. She expressed delight at the rise of farmers' mar-kets that gave others around the country the chance to do what she had done as a girl, and had sought to do all her life: Eat fresh, cook fresh. "One of the greatest pleasures of my life has been that I have never stopped learning about cooking and good food," she said.

JUNE PLATT

June Platt was, in James Beard's estimation, "undoubtedly one of the most important gastronomic authorities this country has produced" and a woman who "occupies a place of honor in American cookery, in the company of the great ladies of the 19th and early 20th century who paved the way in culinary taste."

She was also a bit of a pip, lively and funny and "no gastronomic snob," said Beard, who had lunch with her at the Four Seasons in New York the day Alfred Knopf Jr.—he was at the table too—assigned her to write what turned out to be her last book, *June Platt's New England Cook Book*. This was in the late 1960s, when they spelled cookbook as two words.

Thrilled by the assignment, she rode the train home to Little Comp-ton, Rhode Island, where she lived with her husband in the Cherry Cottage, so named because when they moved in they planted two cherry trees near the front door as an expression of hope and opti-mism. The trees died, but their optimism remained.

Her library at the Cherry Cottage contained six hundred cookbooks, which she looked through for ideas and recipes. She did this quite happily, because in recent years she had been cooking mainly French and so it was a treat "to concentrate instead on Slumps and Toots and Dowdys, to say nothing of Grunts and Buckles and Fannie Daddies."

Her research included her own articles for *House & Garden* and other publications, dating back to the 1930s.

Platt gave lively and fun dinner parties, consistent with her personality, including the one where she bought ten fresh lobsters and stored them in a tub of water in her backyard, not knowing they needed to be kept on ice or in running salt water. The lobsters all died, but she saved the day by finding some cans of tuna in her pantry. She also had on hand Parmesan cheese and fresh brown Rhode Island Red eggs, and she whipped up tuna fish omelets for her guests, based on a Brillat-Savarin recipe.

The recipes in *New England Cook Book* reached back three hundred years, but only one of them was for baked beans, and it is Vermont Baked Beans not Boston. She told how to make home-corned beef, homemade jellies, and beet wine, and the first recipe in "Soups and Chowders" was Daniel Webster's personal recipe for fish chowder. In the 1840s, when the South and North appeared ready to split the Union in two, Webster of Massachusetts and Henry Clay of Kentucky both argued in the Senate to keep the nation together, and their argument carried the day. A Platt family heirloom was the crystal pitcher Webster and Clay used to drink beer from during those Senate debates.

Knopf published *June Platt's New England Cook Book* in 1971, thirty-five years after the publication of her first book, *The June Platt Party Cook Book*. Another classic from this plain and fancy woman was the *Plain and Fancy Cook Book*.

HELEN EVANS BROWN

Helen Evans Brown lived in Julia Child's former hometown of Pasadena and had a cookbook library that dwarfed June Platt's (and probably even Julia's): five thousand books. James Beard thought she was

as good a prose stylist as M. F. K. Fisher, although he and Brown were dear friends and this may have colored his opinion somewhat.

A former caterer and restaurant cook, Brown wrote for *Sunset, McCall's,* and *House & Garden,* and her best book was the *West Coast Cook Book,* which influenced Beard. In it she collected recipes from California, Oregon, and Washington, and he used it as a model for *American Cookery,* his historical compilation of recipes from around the country. After *West Coast Cook Book* came out, Beard wrote her a fan letter, she wrote back, their friendship blossomed, and they became pen pals, exchanging hundreds of gossipy letters over the years about food, cooking, and their personal lives.

When Beard, who constantly fretted about his weight, wrote, "I am getting so fat that I can hard move around," Brown commiserated, replying, "I, too, am poor and fat. What a world!" The two heartily disliked, as Beard put it, food that "imitated" food, and they both enjoyed sleuthing around for obscure cookbooks such as *The Web-Foot Cook Book,* a nineteenth-century cookbook published by the First Presbyterian Church of Portland, Oregon.

She gave him West Coast fish recipes and advice as needed, such as the time he asked about hibachis. He had never seen one and had been told that you did not cook on them but only used them for heat. She said yes, you can use them for warming your hands, but that Japanese families made tea and cooked on them. Brown's writing featured Japanese, Chinese, Mexican, Russian, and Italian recipes, introducing these cuisines to many Americans and in this way prefiguring the coming national interest in the cooking and foods of other countries.

In 1963 Beard wrote to her, "I am worried about you, and really worried. You must take it easy and try not to overdo." His worry was well-

founded. She was suffering from kidney disease, and by November of the next year, just after her good friend flew to Pasadena to see her for the last time, she was dead. She was sixty. Her husband Philip, also a close friend of Beard's and a lover of sumptuous good food himself, finished up the magazine assignments she was working on at the time.

FANNIE FARMER

"I have no patience with cooks who just boil their vegetables, instead of putting heart and soul into cooking so it becomes enjoyable instead of a drudgery," wrote Fannie Farmer, who poured her whole heart and soul into her cooking and who expected others, including her students at the classes she taught in New England, to do the same. In her classes, after the students had made a dish, she asked them to ask themselves, "Could it be better?"

This was what inspired Farmer—the idea of making it better. When she went out to eat, if she liked what she was having, she would put a little bit of it in her handkerchief and bring it home to see if she could match it in her kitchen. When she heard that a French ship had sunk anchor in Boston, she went down to the harbor for a visit. A French ship always carried a French chef, and she wanted to talk to him to learn what she could and taste a little bit of what he was making.

The Boston Cooking School Cookbook—updated for modern readers by Marion Cunningham, a grand American resource in her own right, and renamed *The Fannie Farmer Cookbook*—was first published in 1896. It represented a breakthrough in American cooking. Clocks and timepieces barely existed in most ordinary kitchens, and cooks left instructions in their recipes, such as "You will know it is cooked when it sticks to the spoon" or "Cook for no more than two Our Fathers." Farmer blew away this antiquated approach by emphasizing precise

measurements and standardizing measurements; she was known as "the mother of level measurements."

She also disliked bad bread; she thought good bread essential for good nutrition. She advised her readers on how to judge fresh fish, choose the best cuts of meat, and to stay away from what were called "cooking eggs," older eggs that many bought because they were cheaper. Buy fresh, she told them.

"There's been a lot of talk throughout most of this century about getting the poor housewife out of the kitchen and freeing her from the dreadful menial task of cooking," wrote Cunningham about Farmer. "But Fannie knew the secret—that if you put heart and soul into cooking, you will find tremendous satisfaction."

ELIZA LESLIE

The cookbook author that Fannie Farmer read was Eliza Leslie, the most influential cookery writer of her time. Her 1851 classic, *Miss Eliza's Directions for Cookery*, went through sixty editions, and homemakers and cooks all across the country had dog-eared copies of it in their kitchens.

Born in Philadelphia, Leslie was of Scottish descent; her great grandfather came here before the American Revolution, and her watchmaker father befriended two men who helped set that Revolution in motion, Ben Franklin and Thomas Jefferson. Bright and exceptionally well-read—by age twelve she had powered through Gibbon's history of Rome and all six volumes of James Cook's voyages around the world—she spent her early years in England. But after she returned to America, tragedy struck: Her father died, leaving the family destitute. To make ends meet they ran a boarding house and Eliza went to a cooking school taught by a Mrs. Goodfellow. Mrs. Goodfellow's lessons and her pupil's enthusiasm and talents led to her first book,

MASTER CAKEMAKER

Wayne Thiebaud is the true ace of cakes; he makes cakes that are too good to eat. He has elevated the act of making cakes—and pies and cupcakes—from craft into a form of high art.

Of course, Thiebaud is a painter, not a baker. Details, details.

Ah but what a painter he is! If you love eating cakes and pies and pastries, you will surely love to view, with mouthwatering pleasure, "Pie Slice," a Thiebaud painting of a creamy piece of pie that could be lemon meringue, except the filling is a vivid pink, or "Pies, Pies, Pies," gorgeous rows of apple, chocolate cream, pumpkin, and lemon meringue pies in a pastry case.

"When you think of it, pie is just a triangle," says Thiebaud. "Cakes are circles. I am interested in very, very basic shapes—triangles, half-circles, rectangles."

He is also very interested, one feels safe to say, in the lush beauty of simple food. His mother Alice—another food-related Alice!—loved to cook and bake, and Thiebaud's richly layered and textured canvases of bacon and eggs, barbecued beef sandwiches, hamburgers, birthday cakes, and candy apples are informed, in part, by his memories as a boy in his mother's kitchen and on family picnics in Southern California where he grew up.

Thiebaud came into his own as a painter in the Pop Art era of Andy Warhol, whose "Campbell's Soup Cans" may be the most famous American food paintings ever. But Thiebaud's work is far more inviting, yet with thought-provoking qualities too. "There are layers beneath the layer cakes," was the way Allan Stone put it.

It was Stone's one-man exhibit of Thiebaud's work in 1962 at his Upper East Side gallery that introduced him to the New York art world and springboarded his career. The Stone Collection in New York and Paul Thiebaud Gallery in San Francisco are two dealers that represent his work. Wouldn't that be an impressive moment, inviting your friends over for the unveiling of an original Thiebaud hanging on your living room wall? "Pies" sold at a Sotheby's auction a few years ago for four million dollars.

75 Receipts for Pastry, Cakes and Sweetmeats, which came out in 1828 and was still in print a half a century later.

Leslie wrote voluminously, in part to keep the wolf away but also because she entertained serious literary ambitions. She wrote novels and short stories, and less seriously, those "receipt books," which are why we know her today. They contained advice on frying, stewing, and fricasseeing rabbits; pies of every description—pork, ham, partridge, goose; ochre, oxtail, and mock turtle or calf's head soup; Indian pudding (baked and boiled); potato snow; rusk; how to lard and preserve cream; federal cakes; election cakes; a Sally Lunn cake (named for its inventor); spruce and ginger beer; and gooseberry wine. Despite the antiquarian nature of some of her recipes, her thoughts on cooking and food have a timeless quality:

"Let all housekeepers remember that there is no possibility of producing nice dishes without a liberal allowance of good ingredients."

"A sufficiency of wholesome and well-prepared food is absolutely necessary to the preservation of health and strength, both body and mind."

When Leslie died in 1858, there were seventy editions of her books in print. One hundred fifty years after its original publication, Dover released a modern reprint of *Directions for Cookery*.

THE SNOB 9

CULINARY CLASSES AND SCHOOLS FOR THOSE WHO WISH TO IMPROVE THEIR SKILLS—AND HAVE FUN

Cooking classes for the home chef can be found almost everywhere. They're generally fun, social outings. Nobody goes to a cooking class to have a bad time.

For those who are more serious or career-minded, there are also culinary training schools around the country that offer credential programs in cooking, baking, and other disciplines. May this small sampling of schools and programs inspire you to enroll in a class, learn new knife or butchery skills, and have a good time while you're at it.

CULINARY INSTITUTE OF AMERICA

The CIA is, to borrow from Cole Porter, the Napoleon brandy and Waldorf salad of culinary schools. Its list of graduates includes Charlie Palmer of Aureole, Grant Achatz of Alinea, Susan Feniger of Border Grill, and Roy Choi of Kogi BBQ. It offers multi-year bachelor and associate degrees in the culinary arts as well as Saturday classes and boot camps for home cooks who would like to know how to make better sauces or whip up a tiramisu with confidence. Two amazing CIA campuses are in Hyde Park, New York, on the Hudson River, and

Greystone in St. Helena in the California wine country; there are also branches in San Antonio and Singapore. CIAChef.edu

INSTITUTE OF CULINARY EDUCATION

ICE is the largest culinary training and cooking school in New York City, offering training for foodies of all abilities and professional chefs; *Top Chef* judge Gail Simmons is a graduate. More than twenty-six thousand people take some fifteen hundred classes a year on everything from knife skills and grilling seafood to workshops on West African cuisine and chocolate desserts, taught by the likes of Rick Bayless and Marcus Samuelsson. There are twelve kitchens, six classrooms, a chocolate lab that Willy Wonka would have adored, and fittingly, for an organization known as ICE, a training bar for mixologists. Ice.edu

COOK STREET

Morey Hecox was an Army veteran and attorney who practiced law in New York and Denver for three decades. But all that time he had an itch he couldn't quite scratch—namely, he loved cooking and longed to pursue it in a more serious, full-time way. After retiring from the law, he and Le Cordon Bleu graduate Page Tredennick founded Cook Street, a Denver culinary academy with programs for aspiring pros as well as home cooks. Although Hecox has stepped back from day-to-day operations, Tredennick oversees the school whose teaching philosophy stresses the fundamentals and then builds up from there. CookStreet.com

MIREPOIX

This cooking school is at the Holiday Market in Royal Oak, Michigan, one of the oldest and best produce markets in the Detroit metro area. It's a learn-to-cook and improve-your-skills kind of place, with the emphasis on the social side of things. It hosts bachelorette parties and corporate team-building events in which employees face off

against each other in cooking competitions. Chrysler, Carhartt, and Detroit Diesel are among the Motor City companies that have competed. MirepoixCookingSchool.com

CULINAERIE

Founded by two Susans—Susan C. Holt, who has worked with Michelin two-star chef Gémacrard Pangaud, and Susan Watterson, former director of the culinary program at L'Academie de Cuisine in Bethesda—this Washington, DC school is similar to other leading schools and programs around the country in that it offers a huge variety of classes to choose from. Sample classes: "French Macaron Workshop," "Explore Thai Street Food," "Knife Know-how for Vegetarians," "Sabor a Mexico," "Explore Laotian Fare," and "Indian Grilling: North and South." CulinAerie.com

NEW ORLEANS SCHOOL OF COOKING

If you're visiting New Orleans and in the mood to have a little fun on the bayou, give this touristy French Quarter establishment a go. It's run by Kevin Belton, a six-foot-nine, four hundred–pound ex-NFL lineman who learned to cook from his mother and stars on a public television show on Creole food. Local chefs such as Frank Brigtsen of Brigtsen's Restaurant hold cooking demos that mix New Orleans history and folklore with food, and there are hands-on classes that teach how to make beignets, pralines, jambalaya, crawfish pie, and maybe even filé gumbo. NewOrleansSchoolofCooking.com

SAN FRANCISCO COOKING SCHOOL

The home of the San Francisco Cooking School has a unique history. Located at 690 Van Ness Avenue, one of the city's major boulevards, in 1910 it housed an auto dealership on what was then San Francisco's Auto Row. When the dealership went bust, the Speedo Carburetor Shop took over the building. Then when Speedo cleared out, in

came Jeremiah Tower, who started a new concept restaurant called Speedo 690 in homage to the previous tenant.

But the restaurant business is, as we all know, a fickle thing. After Tower's concept died, food author Jodi Liano was looking around for a place to set up a cooking school, and what could be better than the former home of Speedo 690? She is now director and an occasional teacher at the school, which offers career training and recreational cooking classes. SFCooking.com

THE CAMBRIDGE SCHOOL OF CULINARY ARTS

The CSCA began originally as a continuing ed program for working chefs in the Boston area who needed to keep their kitchen skills sharp while learning new ones. But demand was so high that it expanded its curriculum to include professional training for students hoping to make a career in the food industry. Graduates include James Beard Best Chef nominee Karen Akunowicz of Myers + Chang and Marcos Sanchez at Tasting Counter in Boston. The pastry classes are big hits; they're taught by Delphin Gomes, a French-trained master pastry chef. CambridgeCulinary.com

COOK

There are many reasons why we like Cook. It has a hip urban vibe in downtown Philadelphia on South Twentieth Street. Its demonstration kitchen is small—sixteen seats—and intimate, perfect to get up close and personal with the chef who is cooking that night. A different chef from around the city comes in every night, cooks up a storm, and then the lucky guests get to sample the fruits of his labor. Diners take pictures, write notes, ask questions, and engage in lots of fun, instructive banter with the man or woman at the stove.

"It's like dinner theater without all the cheesiness," says Peter Woolsey of Bistrot La Minette, a Philly chef who has appeared at Cook. Two more are Georges Perrier, the French-born and -trained chef recognized by his native country as a master of haute cuisine, and Aimee Olexy of Talula's Table, one of the hardest dining reservations to get in town. After the meal the guests can shop the gift store or perhaps even buy a cookery book at Cook's vast bookstore. Call us biased, but we're partial to places that sell books. AudreyClaireCook.com

FOODIE SNOB QUIZ #4

COOKBOOKS

"Cookbooks are as alike as brothers. The best is the one you write yourself," said Fernand Point, who wrote a pretty good one himself, *Ma Gastronomie*, a classic of French cuisine.

This chapter's quiz tests your knowledge of the brotherhood and sisterhood of cookbooks. The cookbooks mentioned here differ in many ways but all share the common purpose of showing people how to make good food. Answers follow the quiz.

1. Jeremiah Tower said that if you had to have only one cookbook, *Joy of Cooking* would be it. He would add, however, one more cookbook that he would describe as fundamental for today's cooks. What is it?

    a. *How to Cook Everything,* Mark Bittman
    b. *Essentials of Classic Italian Cooking*, Marcella Hazan
    c. *The Art of Simple Food*, Alice Waters
    d. *Encyclopedia of Asian Food*, Charmaine Solomon

2. In Martin Yang's *Chinatown Cooking*, based on his PBS television series, he tells the fascinating story of the Sam Sui women cooks of Singapore. They ran a popular restaurant and were famous for the box-like red hats they wore. But upon their deaths they asked that an unusual thing be done with their recipes. What was it?

    a. bury their recipes in their graves with them, so they could take them to the afterlife
    b. burn all their recipes with their belongings, for the same reason
    c. publish them posthumously in a cookbook (which occurred, and it became a best seller in Asia)
    d. bury them in a box at a hidden location in the hills, setting off a nationwide treasure hunt to find them

3. *American Cookery*, by Amelia Simmons, is widely considered to be the first cookbook published in the United States. But it was not published the year of the Louisiana Purchase, the year the Constitution was ratified, or the year Abraham Lincoln was born. What was its pub date?

    a. 1809
    b. 1803
    c. 1796
    d. 1787

4. One of these people was the first black astronaut in space. One was the first black to attend the University of Mississippi. One became the first black to win the Wimbledon tennis title. But who wrote *The House Servant's Directory*, published in 1827, the first cookery book with recipes by a black American?

   a. James Meredith

   b. Guion Bluford Jr.

   c. Robert Roberts

   d. Althea Gibson

5. Though they have different cooking and entertaining styles, Ina Garten and Martha Stewart are both best-selling cookbook authors. Three of these statements are by Stewart, one by the somewhat more casual Garten. Which one did Garten say?

   a. "Another reason I love hors d'oeuvres is because they are so beautiful to look at."

   b. "Finicky eaters. There's one at every party."

   c. "The only steadfast rule when composing these edibles—the bread *must* be very very thinly sliced and must be *crustless*!"

   d. "Kathy loves wine, and only white French Burgundies were served at this party."

6. Judith Jones was the extraordinary Knopf editor who shepherded the cookbooks of Julia Child, Marcella Hazan, Madhur Jaffrey, Edna Lewis, Marion Cunningham, and Jacques Pepin. That is certainly true. But of these next four statements, only one is true. Which is it?

   a. She edited Harper Lee's *To Kill a Mockingbird*.

   b. She discovered *Anne Frank: The Diary of a Young Girl* and pushed for its American publication.

   c. She lives at the same Central Park West address as Bobby Flay.

   d. She served with Julia Child in the O.S.S., the Allied intelligence gathering service during World War II.

7. Nora Ephron called them "the holy trinity" of cookbooks, the ones every home cook in the mid-1960s had to have. One was Julia's *Mastering the Art of French Cooking*, the other Craig Claiborne's *The New York Times Cookbook*. What was the third?

a. *Betty Crocker Cookbook*

b. *The James Beard Cookbook*

c. *Better Homes and Gardens Cookbook*

d. *Michael Field's Cooking School*

8. Julee Rosso and Sheila Lukins once ran a tiny yet hugely influential Manhattan gourmet foods shop called The Silver Palate. The preface of their cookbook, also influential in its time, begins with a Brillat-Savarin aphorism: "The discovery of a new dish does more for the happiness of mankind than the discovery of a new star." Here are four more quotes—three by Brillat-Savarin, one by author Virginia Woolf. Which one did Woolf say?

a. "The world is nothing without life, and all that lives takes nourishment."

b. "The pleasures of the table belong to all times and all ages, to every country and every day."

c. "To entertain a guest is to make yourself responsible for his happiness so long as he is beneath your roof."

d. "One cannot think well, love well, sleep well, if one has not dined well."

9. *Thug Kitchen: Eat Like You Give a F**k* is a popular vegetarian cookbook and website whose mission is to "inspire motherf***kers to eat some goddamn vegetables." Its foul-mouthed "thug" authors remained anonymous until an enterprising Epicurious writer revealed their identities. Who are they?

a. roadies in Kanye West's touring show

b. a thirty-something couple in Hollywood

c. elderly Baptist ladies raising money for their Atlanta church

d. members of the American Olympic bobsled team and their coach

10. Eric Ripert called it "the most magnificent book you can find anywhere in the world." It totaled 2,720 pages, weighed nearly ten pounds, contained the recipes of an acclaimed chef, and came with a guidebook on how to find his restaurant. Who was the author?

a. Ferran Adriá

b. Jiro Ono

c. Joël Robuchon

d. Thomas Keller

Answers: 1. a; 2. b; 3. c; 4. c; 5. b; 6. b; 7. d; 8. d; 9. b Matt Holloway and Michelle Davis; 10. a

CHAPTER FIVE

Stars, stars, and more stars

THE LIFE OF A FOODIE

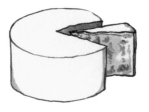

The life of a foodie begins at home with the food she eats and cooks. It hardly stops there, though. That's only the beginning in many ways. As Regina Schrambling wrote, with her creative spelling, "Fud people wanna talk fud, that's it." And what, exactly, do fud people talk about when they talk fud? Rock star chefs, the best places to get English muffins or sushi or almond cookies, what that nasty critic said, what's trending (or not), and possibly how many stars a restaurant has. We'll talk about all these things in this chapter and spell all the words correctly.

7 REASONS WHY ROY CHOI IS HIPPER THAN YOU

HE'S A BETTER COOK TOO

If there is anyone who embodies the phrase "Rock Star Chef," it is Roy Choi. He is the Korean-born LA celebrity chef and restaurateur whose Kogi BBQ taco trucks basically launched the gourmet food truck craze.

However hip you are—and you are no doubt EXTREMELY hip since you are reading this book—you are not as hip as Roy. Sorry, nothing personal, it's just a fact. Here is why.

1. ROY CHOI REPRESENTS.

Roy is all LA—and proud of it. When he wears a ball cap—turned sideways and set slightly back on his head, naturally—it is often the cap of his hometown Los Angeles Dodgers. From time to time he even sports their colors, blue and white.

Choi comes by his allegiance honestly. Growing up in the Koreatown District of LA, he and other Korean kids and their families would go out to Chavez Ravine to watch the Dodgers play. After the game— or around the sixth or seventh inning; Dodgers fans are notorious

for leaving games early to beat the traffic—everyone would pile into their cars and head back over to Eighth Street in K-Town to have noodles, kimchi, and short ribs at Dong Il Jang.

2. ROY CHOI SAYS "MUTHAF**KA" A LOT.

In his autobiography *L.A. Son*, written with Natasha Phan and Tien Nguyen, Choi swears a lot, which, like arm sleeves, appears to be a job requirement for young and edgy chefs today. David Chang curses in media interviews; so does the graying Anthony Bourdain. It shows them as men of the street, savvy and sharp-edged, who are no longer afraid that their mother is going to wash their mouth out with soap for saying bad words.

Choi's favorite swear word without doubt is *muthaf**ka*. Note the spelling—mother not with an *o* but with a *u*. He also drops the conventional *er* for an *a*, and then ends it all with a flourish with another *a*. Choi can pull this off because he has street cred and—here we use the term as he does, as a compliment of the highest order—a bad muthaf**ka. So are, in his judgment, the LA food scene—"that muthaf**kin' LA food"—his father—"a badass muthaf**ka"—himself during his out-of-control gambling days—"I was a king, right? El muthaf**kin' Rey"—and Chef Ron DeSantis, who oversaw the Culinary Institute of America in Hyde Park when Choi studied there—"a certified master chef, a former military chef, a badass muthaf**ka."

SNOB ASIDE

Muthaf**kas aside, one should never forget that Choi is a superbly trained chef and a great admirer of the craft of cooking and those, like Jacques Pepin, who have come before him. "Reading Pepin made me realize how little I actually knew about the craft of cooking," confessed Choi in his early apprentice days as a cook. "Jacques Pepin became my Mr. Miyagi as he slowed the process down and showed me that cooking takes time, dedication, and practice, practice."

3. ROY CHOI QUOTES BRUCE LEE.

For his book's epigraph Choi does not draw from Brillat-Savarin or Escoffier or Marie-Antoine Carême (whose work he came to know at the CIA) or some other traditional if stodgy French name. Instead he cites two quotations from Bruce Lee, which is about as dope as it gets:

"For it is easy to criticize and break down the spirit of others, but to know yourself takes a lifetime."

"The possession of anything begins in the mind."

4. ROY CHOI HAS STRUGGLED WITH DEMONS.

Nothing lends street cred to a chef like a goatee (check), tattoos (check check), and battles with addictions and personal demons (check, check, check—the hat trick!). Roy Choi has all three.

In his life he has done drugs, had a brief destructive fling with crack cocaine, drunk himself blind, stolen from his parents to support his vices, and gambled so hard—he once won a thirty-four thousand–dollar Texas Hold 'Em hand and would regularly cash out with a grand in his pocket after nightly games in K-Town, money he'd then throw away at the clubs and on women and drugs and partying till dawn—that when the inevitable crash came, it ended with his parents and friends doing an intervention on him to save his life.

5. ROY CHOI HAS HAD AN EMERIL MOMENT.

All successful chefs have a mentor or mentors, people who give them a boost when they are young and finding their way. Roy Choi is no different. One of his mentors was Eric Ripert, who hired him to work for Le Bernardin after he left Hyde Park and was looking for experience in a big-time New York restaurant. Nobody else would give him a job, but Ripert saw something he liked and installed him in his Michelin three-star kitchen. Another mentor was Rokusaburo Michiba, the

Japanese sushi master (and the first Iron Chef; he trained Morimoto), whom Choi apprenticed under for a time in Tokyo.

But none of these extraordinary opportunities would have ever happened if Choi, suffering through another bad phase in his life, fighting others and himself and drinking and depressed, had not clicked on the TV one morning in a hangover stupor and seen Emeril Lagasse doing a cooking show. It was a revelation, the proverbial thunderbolt from on high. What Emeril was doing, Choi realized, he could do too. Not the television part necessarily, but the cooking part.

"That was it. I made up my mind. I was done with the anger, the shame, the mistakes, the self pity, the pain." Done with all that, and finally ready to get serious about his calling. Bam!

6. ROY CHOI IS A GREAT AMERICAN IMMIGRANT SUCCESS STORY.

Choi was born in South Korea, and so were his parents. He is 100 percent American. Besides his affection for the Dodgers, he was a Cub Scout. His father ordered him to memorize English words at night in his room, and his father and mother strictly enforced the rule of only speaking English in the home so their son could thrive outside the home in school or business or whatever he was doing.

Even so, his parents suffered hard times and discrimination in their adopted country. His father, who has a master's degree from the University of Pennsylvania, owned a liquor store that he sold. Then his parents ran a Korean restaurant in LA that failed. But it all worked out in the end, because eventually they entered the jewelry business and absolutely nailed that American Dream thing. They became millionaires, saying good-bye to Koreatown and buying an Orange County mansion that was once owned by Nolan Ryan, the Hall of Fame pitcher.

And their son, well, he's doing okay on that American Dream thing too.

7. ROY CHOI IS A CAR GUY.

Being totally LA, Choi is a total car guy. Deal with it. No bug-like Google robot cars for him. When he explains what he loves about the city, he talks about how you need to "roll down your window and smell the sweet dripping of lechón and carne asada smoking in the back-yards" and how when you drive through K-Town "the smoke from the Korean BBQ grills sticks to your hair for days no matter which fancy shampoo you choose" and then going to some cafe where you can "wash down your beers with crispy Korean fried chicken." All you need to complete the picture is Snoop Dogg or Tupac laying down the background tunes.

The teenaged Choi drove an '87 Chevy Blazer—white with gold trim, blacked-out windows, fuzzy dice hanging on the rearview mirror, building-shaking sound system—and rolled with a crew of lowriders known as the Street City Minis, the only Asian dude among Chicanos. Choi's career breakthrough as an adult also owes a great deal to the internal combustion engine. This came during another down-in-the-dumps period after he had been fired from a chef's job. A friend of his, Mark Manguera, who knew Choi from when they had worked together at the Beverly Hilton, called him to pitch him with an idea. When they got together in person, over lattes and cigarettes, Manguera laid it out for him, in all its brilliant and bodacious simplicity.

Korean BBQ in a taco.

"Wouldn't it be delicious?" he said.

Cue Emeril: Bam! The two of them went to work the next day, cruising Kaju Market in Koreatown for ingredients and going back to Manguera's apartment to start putting it together, bit by bit, piece by piece. Maybe it wasn't art, but what they were making tasted really, really good, and in the fall of 2008, just before Thanksgiving, Choi climbed

in behind the wheel of a big 1980s-era Grumman catering truck, the original #69, and drove to Silver Lake in Los Angeles, parked it on the street, and introduced those badass muthaf**kin' tacos to a world in dire need of them.

ROY CHOI'S LA DINING PICKS

Los Angeles is a great restaurant city. If you doubt this, just ask Roy Choi, who has eaten all over the city and knows its food scene perhaps better than anyone. Here are a few of his top picks.

- **Dong Il Jang.** This is a grand, old-school Koreatown institution, not a place for Korean BBQ but more traditional fare. Choi took Anthony Bourdain there for an episode of *Parts Unknown*. LA food bloggers Kevin Cheng and Barbara Hansen liked the *yook hwe* (beef sashimi) and roast *gui* (sliced and grilled rib eye), respectively.
- **Phoenix Bakery.** Another old-school institution, this one a Chinatown bakery. Founded in the late 1930s by Fung Chow Chan and his wife Wai Hing, the Chan family still runs it. Choi loves the almond cookies. Also worth a taste: the sticky sugar butterfly pastries and wintermelon cakes. PhoenixBakeryInc.com
- **Border Grill.** Mary Sue Milliken and Susan Feniger's gourmet Mexican restaurant that, says Choi correctly, "helped put Mexican food on the national map." Originally on Melrose, it long ago moved to Santa Monica and there are now locations around LA and Las Vegas. BorderGrill.com
- **Matsuhisa.** This was the Beverly Hills restaurant where Choi first tasted the new style of sashimi as prepared by Nobuyuki Matsuhisa, better known as Nobu. After Matsuhisa opened to rave reviews, Robert DeNiro urged Nobu to take the concept to New York City, which he did. The brand has gone worldwide. NobuMatsuhisa.com
- **LaBrea Bakery.** When it opened, and when Choi first started going here, it offered six kinds of artisan breads: sourdough baguette, country white sourdough, whole wheat, Normandy rye, olive, and rosemary olive oil. Soon after that it won a blind tasting for "Best French Bread" in LA, and some still think this is true. LaBrea Bakery.com
- More favorites of Choi's: The Dragon, Soot Bull Jeep, Mom's Place, Kobawoo House—all Korean places in K-Town—and Hurry Curry, a Japanese curry spot across town on Sawtelle Boulevard, "a little street with some of the best ramen and sushi in the country," he says.

SEEING STARS

A SNOB Q&A ON HOW TO MAKE SENSE OF THE MICHELIN STAR RATING SYSTEM

Roy Choi would be the first to testify about the high-pressure, high-stakes life of a chef. Turning covers night after night while dealing with meddling management, unreliable staff, petulant customers, and, oh yeah, those irksome critics and their stars. Ah those stars!

Those tiny five-pointed objects attached to a restaurant review can represent giant galactic death stars for a chef, especially if it is the Michelin Guide that is issuing them. Michelin's stars are the most influential on the planet, and yet there is still considerable confusion on how they operate. Please allow us to sort it all out for you in this handy Q&A format:

Q: Why focus on Michelin? There are lots of sites and publications that rate restaurants.

The Snob: True. The *New York Times* has a four-star rating system, and it is the review that counts the most in New York. Other news-

papers and publications have developed their own star systems, such as the *Dallas Morning News* with its top rating of five. Yelp has five stars. The West Coast–centered AAA, which, like Michelin, started as a travel guide for motorists and has branched into restaurant and hotel reviews, eschews stars for diamonds, five diamonds being the best. Zagat uses a thirty-point rating system; Gault and Millau, a French guide, has a twenty-point scale. Even the French government has gotten into the act; *La Liste*, its ratings guide, has developed a one hundred–point scale. The World's 50 Best Restaurants, headquartered in London, is another influential ratings guide, competing with La Liste and Gault and Millau in Europe.

Q: So why Michelin then?

The Snob: Because, to quote Paul Bocuse, "Michelin is the only guide that counts" in haute cuisine. Of course Bocuse may be a little partial in this regard, because his Lyon restaurant has received Michelin's top rating every year since 1965, the longest consecutive three-star run in global gastronomic history. A former Michelin inspector who wrote a tell-all book about the company said that the Guide favored Bocuse, a charge denied by Michelin. But it does somewhat defy credulity to believe that a restaurant can maintain the highest standards, without fail, year after year after year, with nary a hiccup. Can you imagine being the inspector who walked into the conference room at Michelin in France to argue that L'Auberge du Pont de Collonges should lose one of its stars? That is why the French invented the guillotine.

Q: That last joke may not be entirely in good taste. Didn't a French chef kill himself because his restaurant lost a star?

The Snob: Well no, not exactly. But the larger point is, *le guide rouge* must be taken seriously because it can make or break careers and

SNOB ADVICE

The best advice on how to choose a restaurant is to look at a variety of sources. Michelin, the newspaper, these other guides—they can all be useful. See how many reviews there are of a given place on Yelp or Chowhound; if only a few, the reviews may not be credible. The more reviews there are, typically, the better you can assess what people are saying. Jane and Michael Stern's *Roadfood* is another place to look. Any old *Gourmets* sitting around the house? They have reviews too.

boost the bottom line. Eric Ripert said that Le Bernardin recorded a 20 percent jump in sales after being awarded three stars from Michelin, a designation it still holds. And once a restaurant lands that exalted rating, the chef feels enormous pressure to maintain it because of the stakes involved.

Q: Is that why that chef killed himself?

The Snob: Again, that is not precisely correct. He did not kill himself because of a lost star, as some think. The truth is more complicated than that. First we must specify which French chef we're talking about. In 1990 Alain Chapel, one of the inventors of nouvelle cuisine, suffered a fatal heart attack at age fifty-two—caused in part, it was said, by the pressures of running a restaurant with a Michelin three-star ranking. The year after his death, his restaurant lost a star.

Benoît Violier is a more recent case. He was the executive chef of the Hotel de Ville in Crissier, Switzerland; La Liste ranked it No. 1 in the world. (No. 2 that year was Thomas Keller's Per Se.) The French-born Violier was utterly devoted to haute cuisine. "It's my life," he said. "I go to sleep with cooking. I wake up to cooking." But one day in early 2016 he woke up and shot himself with a hunting rifle. He was forty-four years old, married, and had children, but apparently he was

troubled by the recent deaths of his father and his mentor, the chef Philippe Rochat, as well as the pressures of the life he so loved. Hotel de Ville had three Michelin stars at the time of his death, and it still has three Michelin stars.

But the most notorious incident, and one that is still being debated, with considerable heat, involved Bernard Loiseau, a French chef who killed himself in 2003. His suicide surely influenced *Ratatouille*, the delightful Pixar movie about a rat who becomes a chef at a high-end Paris restaurant. The rat draws his inspiration from Auguste Gusteau, the chef-owner who fell into a funk and died after his restaurant lost one of its coveted stars. The fictional Gusteau resembles the real-life Loiseau tragedy.

Q: What happened?

The Snob: Well, again, it's very sad, as all these stories are. Loiseau was fifty-two years old, had three children, and was one of the most famous and successful chefs in France when he died. His restaurant was La Cote d'Or in Burgundy—*trés* expensive ($275 for a chicken dish alone) and very highly regarded but reportedly living off past glories rather than doing the new and creative things sought by critics and diners. Twenty points being the top, Gault and Millau knocked La Cote down to seventeen points, a hard fall. But even more ominous were the rumors about the beating that Michelin was about to deliver. Francois Simon, food critic for *Le Figaro,* the influential Paris daily, wrote that Michelin was thinking about dropping one of Loiseau's three stars and making it merely a two-star establishment. Simon's report appeared February 24, 2003. Two days later Loiseau put a bullet in his head.

They're still pointing fingers as to who is to blame. Michelin denies responsibility, noting how La Cote d'Or maintained its three-star rat-

ing the year of Loiseau's death and retained it for the next thirteen years. (It was finally demoted to two in 2016.) The critic Simon thinks this lets Michelin off far too easily though, saying that the guide issued a private warning to Loiseau and his wife that La Cote was in trouble and that it needed to do better—or else. Still, Simon is unrepentant. He believes the chef had indeed lost his edge and by reporting what people were saying he was just doing his job. "Loiseau was used to a press that acted like courtesans in front of the king," he told a reporter. "I ate at La Cote d'Or, didn't find it glorious and had been hearing others say the same."

Loiseau's widow Dominique isn't buying it. She has charged Simon and other French writers with publishing false rumors, and that their reports triggered a sudden change in her husband's mood and led to his death. "It is from this moment that his behavior began to change, to become incomprehensible. We couldn't reason with him. He was convinced the media wanted his skin." Adding, "Bernard suffered under the media pressure."

Q: It so often comes down to that, doesn't it? The chefs and restaurants versus the critics.

The Snob: It's true. The chefs and restaurants put their hearts and souls into what they do, and then they get dissed by someone who may or may not know anything about food. It hurts them personally and it affects their livelihood, and it's terribly unfair, in their view. On the other hand, these reviews do provide a useful service. For instance, that famous Pete Wells review of Per Se in the *Times* cost nearly three thousand dollars for dinner for four. That's a lot of money for people to just walk in cold without having some inkling of what they're getting into—not only how much they're going to spend, but what the food and service and ambience are like. Plus, who wouldn't

rather read an entertaining, well-done hit job than a piece of public relations puffery?

Q: By the way, how many stars did the *Times* give Per Se?

The Snob: Two. It knocked it down from its former top rating of four.

MATCH GAME 3

STAR CHEFS AND THEIR MENTORS: UNLOCK THE SECRET!

All great chefs have a person or persons who deeply influenced their cooking, giving them their first big break in the business or training them when they were young.

But it's not always predictable who these mentors are, which may make this match game challenging for some. Match the well-known chef or foodie on the left with the mentor on the right. But there's a secret to figuring out this puzzle. Focus on the ones you know, and that will lead you to quickly unlock the rest of the answers. The answers are buried like hidden treasure on p. 179.

Chef	Mentor
Mario Batali Babbo	Jeremiah Tower Stars
Grant Achatz Alinea	Thomas Keller The French Laundry
Ina Garten "Barefoot Contessa"	Martha Stewart Martha Stewart Living
Christopher Kostow Restaurant at Meadowood	Daniel Humm Eleven Madison Park
Wolfgang Puck Spago	Raymond Thuilier Baumaniere
Dan Barber Blue Hill	David Bouley Bouley
Bobby Flay Mesa Grill	Jonathan Waxman Barbuto
Alice Waters Chez Panisse	Cecilia Chang The Mandarin
Daniel Boulud Daniel	Paul Bocuse L'Auberge du Pont de Collonges
Wylie Dufresne Wd-50	Jean-Georges Vongerichten Jean-Georges

LONE STAR STATE FEUD

DALLAS RESTAURANTS
BATTLE A FOOD CRITIC

It started with a trick, and it set off one of the nastiest food critic–restaurant fights we have ever heard of.

The man behind the trick was Michael Martensen, a bartender, uh sorry, mixologist, of renown in Dallas and the owner of Proof + Pantry in the One Arts Plaza neighborhood of the city. Fed up with the critiques of Leslie Brenner, the restaurant reviewer for the *Dallas Morning News*, he decided to blow the cover off one of her most cherished self-beliefs: her (supposed) anonymity.

For years Brenner, an author and former *Los Angeles Times* critic, had functioned on the premise that the chefs and waitstaffs and restaurant managers she encountered did not know who she was, that her identity was a mystery like what happened to Malaysian Flight 370. This was, of course, fiction; restaurant people had IDed her long ago. The fine dining scene in Dallas, like every city, is a small world; chefs know other chefs, bartenders know other bartenders, waiters know other waiters, and they get together for drinks and food from time to time. And they call or email or post or tweet the latest gossip.

Dallas restaurateurs freely traded info on Brenner—what she looked like (middle-aged, black curly hair, glasses), who she often dined with

(her husband), and any identifying idiosyncrasies (yes, a telltale one: She and her hubby often spoke French to each other at the table). Brenner herself recognized that her anonymity may have been more pretend than real. Based on how much she ate out (four or five nights a week) and the years she had been doing this for the paper, she knew there would be times when she would be spotted at a restaurant.

Which is precisely what happened. Proof + Pantry had been open only for a couple of months, and Martensen and his staff were waiting for her to appear, expecting her to arrive at some point to taste the food and do a review. The night she did, they sat her and her party in a prime window spot that looked out on the Arts District, an arts, shopping, and restaurant scene in Dallas. But after their meal was over, something shocking occurred—shocking to Brenner, certainly.

Martensen appeared at their table, explained to her that he knew who she was, and that dinner was on the house. No charge. They were his guests, and he hoped they had enjoyed their evening.

Every bit of this was premeditated. Martensen knew the paper's restaurant reviewing policy—that Brenner had to dine anonymously, that the meal had to be paid for, and that she needed to eat there at least twice before filing a review. He had blown her cover and refused payment, negating the first two requirements, and because of that he knew she could not come back a second time. All of this meant no review of Proof + Pantry by Brenner in the paper, which was his goal. TKO Martensen.

Not so fast. Brenner had a few tricks of her own up her sleeve.
After he left their table she and her party sat for a while, discussing what to do. Finally they got up and walked off, exiting the restaurant. When the waitstaff came to clean her table, they had a surprise waiting for them: five hundred dollars, in cash.

Take that, fella. The bill was paid.

The next day Proof + Pantry called the *Morning News* and explained they did not want Brenner's money and would not accept it. The paper refused to take it back. Eventually it was donated to a *Morning News*–sponsored charity.

The news of what happened quickly spread around the Dallas restaurant scene, and Martensen emerged as a folk hero to all those who felt they had been unfairly treated by Brenner in the past. One of them was John Tesar, the chef-owner of the steakhouse Knife who has appeared on *Top Chef*. He once tweeted "F**k you" to Brenner after she left him off a listing of top chefs in the city. He felt she had deliberately ignored Knife because of its popularity, and in retaliation he banned her from his restaurants. "She's a spoiled little child," he said of her.

SNOB ASIDE

One should always keep all this quarreling in perspective. As food writer Jeff Ruby observes, sagely, "The sniping is especially brutal in the food arena, by its nature a bitchy profession. Foodies live for such battles and happily choose sides, while the rest of the world has no idea who these people are or why we care."

Others accused Brenner of favoritism and downgrading a restaurant simply because a chef she liked had left it. Even Pete Wells, no stranger to the hostility of restaurant owners and chefs, waded into the fight, defending her by citing a review for which she'd been attacked. "You can hand that review out to a class of future restaurant critics and say, 'Look at how this was done.' It was thorough as anything. I think she went four times. I just find it mystifying," he said.

Like with Wells, the unhappiness with Brenner stemmed not so much from what she said in her reviews—although this could be rough—but

rather from the stars she awarded (or not). Many chefs and restaurateurs feel they can put up with the criticism, whatever it is, but the stars leave them feeling sucker-punched. It's baffling to them why one place gets one star whereas another of equal stature gets two—or three or none—or why one star is added, or more seriously, one is dropped. It often seems arbitrary and baffling to the public as well, as if the stars are based on the biases and whims of the reviewer.

The *Morning News* and the *Times* (as well as other newspapers and rating services like Michelin) provide brief, somewhat vague explanations of what their stars mean and how they are assigned. This is by design. If they explained in detail their judging criteria and what the specific ingredients for success are, every restaurant would follow those guidelines to get the highest possible rating. And what would be the point of their reviews then? Reviewers also rightly claim editorial privilege—they do not have to explain anything to restaurants if they choose not to. They answer to their readers, and if the stars work for them, that's all that matters. And finally, taste is, after all, subjective. So if there is a subjective quality to the stars, so be it.

Why the stars are so damaging—or rewarding, when they work in your favor—is a simple truism that everyone on both sides of the argument concede: The public may or may not read the review, but all eyes go to those stars. They tell everything a person needs to know in a glance. And as Texas journalist Zac Crain has noted, "Stars mean business travelers. Stars mean money."

One *Morning News* critic gave the Bird Café in Fort Worth two stars, which in the paper's five-star system, equals "good." This struck owner Shannon Wynne as bizarre. "In what universe does two stars equal good?" she asked in disbelief. "A kid can do the math."

Citing the behavior of children may be appropriate in this case, considering how this messy little scrap ended. After being outed by Martensen at Proof + Pantry, Brenner concocted a ruse of her own. Revenge, as the saying goes, is a dish best served cold, and so she waited more than two months before reappearing at the restaurant, determined to eat there again so she could do a review. But this time, knowing that she would be recognized if she and her party showed up as themselves, they all came in costume. Which was perfectly appropriate. It was the night of Halloween.

She came dressed as a mummy, her face obscured by the wrapping around it. And the ruse worked. No one recognized her. Then, when the review was published, it appeared with a picture of her in her mummy costume—her middle finger raised in defiance, flipping the bird to her antagonists.

Brenner has since come out into the open and no longer tries to be anonymous when reviewing a restaurant.

HOW TO SPOT A FOOD CRITIC

A 5-POINT TIP SHEET FOR CHEFS AND RESTAURANTS

Food critics are known to employ a variety of cloak-and-dagger tactics to prevent chefs and restaurants from knowing who they are and why they are actually dining there.

No more. At long last, here is a foolproof five-point restaurant industry guide on how to detect whether or not an enemy food critic has infiltrated your surroundings.

1. NOTE THE DISGUISE.

Costumes and disguises are a favorite technique of cunning reviewers. Ruth Reichl used to create alternative identities for herself—characters she referred to as "Chloe," "Molly," even her mother, who was a real person—and then dressed according to how she thought this character would look if she were going out for dinner.

Reichl has retired as a reviewer but still, if you see someone in your restaurant dressed like the Easter Bunny or Ronald McDonald or a drag queen in *The Adventures of Priscilla, Queen of the Desert*, be very, very suspicious.

2. BE WARY OF ALL STRAIGHT-LOOKING MIDDLE-AGED MALES.

It is a well-known fact that although their identities are cloaked in mystery, Michelin inspectors tend to be middle-aged men who dress conservatively and often dine alone. Bernard Loiseau, that talented and tortured soul, was constantly on the lookout for diners who fit this profile at La Cote d'Or, assessing whether a man in a suit eating alone was secretly a Michelin man assessing him. This was also a subplot in the movie *Burnt*, in which Bradley Cooper, playing a self-absorbed chef, obsessed about Michelin inspectors showing up in his dining room.

You would be advised to adopt the same level of paranoia. Look around your restaurant. See any middle-aged businessmen out there? In a suit perhaps, balding, a bit of a bulge around the midsection, beads of moisture on his pinkish forehead? This could be a dead giveaway, even more so than if he shows up in a Groucho Marx mask.

3. THEY PAY IN CASH.

Restaurant reviewers often pay in cash, because if they hand over a credit card the restaurant has their name and can identify them. So be on the alert for this cash-only stratagem. If a customer pays an $850 dinner tab all in Benjamins, she is almost certainly a restaurant critic or a drug dealer, or possibly both. We say this because of what they're paying in the newspaper business these days. It's *rough*. This is forcing many otherwise law-abiding critics to go Breaking Bad and sell meth or other illegal substances on the side to help send their kids to college and pay their bills. Sad but true. (Well, not really, but it sounds good.)

4. THEY SHOW TOO MUCH CURIOSITY.

A little curiosity among diners is normal. Too much curiosity is a sure sign that the person you're dealing with is a critic, pure and simple.

Observe how devious they are! They ask seemingly innocent questions about the ingredients of the bruschetta or some other aspect of the service or kitchen. These questions are about as innocent as what the Wolf asked Little Red Riding Hood in Grandma's house. The critics may even already know the answers, and the only reason they are asking is to test the knowledge and veracity of the waitstaff. Bastards!

5. THEY ARE REPEAT CUSTOMERS.

Generally, newspapers prefer that a critic eat at a restaurant at least twice before writing about it. So if you miss that snake in the grass the first time, you have a second chance to eyeball him.

Let us review. If diners appear in your establishment more than once, if they ask too many annoying questions, if they are dressed like Wolverine or Lady Gaga in a meat dress, if they are straight and alone—

FIGHTING LIKE CATS AND DOGS

Everybody knows that foodies fight like cats and dogs. Which brings us to yet another area of disagreement: cats and dogs.

A deeply superficial investigation of this issue suggests that food people tend to be cat people. Foodies like dogs, just not as much as they like cats.

Bobby Flay. The chef and television personality showed that he is on top of the feline trend by naming one of his New York City restaurants Gato, which is Spanish for "cat." The story goes that before the restaurant was built, Flay went to the Lafayette Street space to inspect it. An orange tabby cat appeared in the room, giving him the inspiration for the name. The cat has not been seen since.

Andy Ricker. He is the chef of Pok Pok, the wonderful Thai restaurant whose home is in Portland and has branched out to Los Angeles and New York. Ricker is a real softie for strays, and his Instagram feed is littered with selfies of him and cats.

Ruth Reichl. The former *Gourmet* editor has posted pictures of her cats, ZaZa and Cielo, on her blog. No arriviste when it comes to the aren't-cats-hip trend, her love affair with felines goes way back. For her best-selling memoir *Tender at the Bone*, her author bio described her

as living in New York with her husband, son, and "two cats."

Cat Cora. Frankly we do not know if this *Iron Chef America* chef is a cat person or not. But she goes by Cat, which is good enough for us. Her given name is Catherine.

Julia Child. The most famous cat in foodie cat history belonged to Julia and Paul Child. Her name was Minette. She was, said Julia, who adored her, "a mutt, perhaps a reformed alley cat—a sly, gay, mud- and cream-colored little thing." Somewhat like Bobby Flay's stray, Minette showed up uninvited at the Childs' apartment in Paris and quickly ingratiated herself into their lives. She was the first cat Julia ever had, and after they took her in, she started seeing cats all over the city, in alleys and looking down from windows and fire escapes, and she came to equate them with the freedoms and joys of the city itself.

Susanna Reich wrote a charming illustrated children's book on Julia's cat, *Minette's Feast*.

Dog people. In the interests of fair play, one feels obligated to note that yes, foodies love dogs too (as does the Snob!). Bryant Ng is the much-praised Singapore-born chef of The Spice Table in Los Angeles, and his York-

shire terrier "Teddy" is named after Theodore Roosevelt. When Michelin two-star chef Doug Keane (formerly of Cyrus, now of Two Birds/One Stone in Healdsburg) won the *Top Chef Masters* cooking competition, the one hundred thousand dollars in prize money was donated to a nonprofit Sonoma County animal shelter he cofounded. He's a certified dog trainer.

Anita Lo is a first-generation Chinese American and the French-trained owner-chef of Annisa in Greenwich Village. When she comes home after a hard day in the kitchen, two shih tzus, Mochi and Adzuki, are there to greet her in her 450-square-foot apartment. Carole Bergman Kulok and Winston Kulok own

restaurants in New York and Long Island. They are also longtime dog lovers, drawing their inspiration from a Maltese they acquired as a puppy.

See if you can guess this dog's name. The first restaurant the Kuloks opened was Café Henri in Long Island City. Then came Bar Henry in Manhattan. Bar Henry is closed, but Café Henri continues strong, and the Kuloks have a Michelin one-star Mexican restaurant in Long Island City whose name is—drum roll, please—Casa Enrique. Its menu features an illustration of Henri/Henry/Enrique wearing a sombrero. The executive chef there is Cosme Aguilar, a dog lover himself who contributed an organic chicken recipe for a cookbook for dogs.

or if they are in a group and constantly share food from each other's plates—and if they produce a wad of bills as thick as your fist when they pay, you must accept that you have a major emergency on your hands. A food critic and her party have clearly infiltrated your premises, and there is only one thing to do. Treat them like royalty.

OOPS, WE SPILLED THE BEANS!

HOW TO TELL IF A RESTAURANT IS TRENDING

As every foodie will admit, in her more solemn and introspective moments, it's tough chasing the trends. The trends can change as fast as a green light switches to red, and you never want to be caught posting from a restaurant or bar or nightclub that's suddenly blinking red—i.e., no longer trending.

Fortunately, the Snob can help. This is a handy ten-point guide to determine whether or not the place you're going to Friday night is truly *in*, and therefore worthy of your presence.

1. IT'S REINVENTING SOMETHING FOR THE TWENTY-FIRST CENTURY.

One reason the blustery Dallas chef John Tesar was so ticked off at critic Leslie Brenner was that she had neglected to do a review of his Knife steakhouse. "She's ignoring the most popular restaurant in town," he said. "I'm not making that up. I'm blown away by its success. We reinvented the steakhouse in the state of Texas. I mean, it's a real story."

Of course it is. It always is. A steakhouse opening today cannot be just a steakhouse; too boring. It has to be reinvented and reimagined for the twenty-first century. This last is absolutely vital. Always go to a twenty-first-century place, or even a twenty-second century (awesome!) place. Never ever be seen in the twentieth century unless, of course, you're doing a self-consciously retro thing, a la No. 2.

2. IT'S FROM THE *MAD MEN* ERA.

The popularity of *Mad Men* made everything pre-1965 cool: grown-up cocktails, cigarettes, Don Draper's hair and ultra-smooth chin, Joan's Jayne Mansfield curvaciousness, cigarette pants, polka-dot skirts, tucked-in waists, shiny shoes, fedoras. Naturally the trend spilled over into fine dining, where Mario Carbone and his restaurant group are "reinventing" one of the classic old-school restaurant spaces of midtown Manhattan, The Grill Room. It originally opened in 1959 in the *Mad Men* era, and the new Grill Room will refer back to those days in its look, vibe, and cuisine, while keeping everything thoroughly twenty-first century, of course.

This trend comes with a three-alarm warning. *Mad Men* the series is kaput, so its trendiness is heading into perilous seas. Check your local TV listings for a coming restaurant trend near you.

3. IT'S POPPING UP.

Pop-ups are edgy, experimental, ad hoc, theatrical, temporary. They push the envelope, expand the boundaries, stand the clichés on their head. Grant Achatz, he of Michelin three-star Alinea fame, staged one of the best pop-ups we have ever heard of. It started with the waitstaff presenting each diner with a sealed envelope. Upon opening, the note inside said, "Please, shut up."

The dining room then filled with bright light as if from a heavenly source and the first course—white asparagus—arrived on plates of white. Obediently, no one uttered a word as they ate. When they were finished, the room went suddenly dark and Keith Richards's opening guitar riff for "Paint It Black" came over the sound system. One food critic noted with approval that the room was so dark it was hard to tell if he had finished the food on his plate, which is always a good sign. If you can't see the food you're eating, you know you're in a hip spot.

4. THE DISHES HAVE ARTSY NAMES.

The grand Italian chef Massimo Bottura excels at this. Here are actual names of dishes on the menu of Osteria Francescana in Modena: "An eel swimming up the Po River"; "Memory of a mortadella sandwich"; "Beautiful, psychedelic spin-painted veal"; "Autumn in New York" (that's a song too, and a really good one; Sinatra's version is perfect mood music for the reimagined Grill Room); "Misery and Nobility"; "This little piggy went to market"; and perhaps the greatest name for a dessert in the history of fine dining, "Oops! I dropped the lemon tart."

5. THE CHEF IS A MASTER OF MOLECULAR GASTRONOMY.

Everyone knows that molecular gastronomy is dead, or dying, or in a near-death state, or still brilliantly and inventively alive. Nonetheless everyone can agree that it is not as trendy as it was in the glory days of say, 2005. "I do not need a foam version of bacon," food critic Simran Sethi has said dismissively. "Give me the sizzle."

But! As noted earlier, these things can change in a blink. So if molecular gastronomy is dead, or dying, its resurrection will surely be coming soon, and when it does you want to be there first.

6. IT'S POST-INDUSTRIAL.

What this phrase means, in plain language, is this:

If you're chillin' with tapas and a Blind Pig IPA in an old industrial relic that your blue-collar grandfather might have worked in, back in the day, but that has been converted into a stylish new boîte for digital warriors who sit in cubicles staring at screens all day long in an air-conditioned office, and who do not belong to a union but who nevertheless identify with the whole working-class Wobblies' proletariat thing, as well as the grubby, farmyard-gardening-get-your-hands-dirty work-with-the-land thing—although they don't do *that* either—you're *there*.

Examples of these places abound, but Seattle appears to be leading the way. Charles Smith Wines is housed in a former Dr. Pepper bottling plant near an airport. No less than three John Sundstrom places—Lark, Bitter/Raw, and Slab Sandwiches + Pie—have spaces in an ex–auto parts warehouse that opened when Model Ts were all the rage. Nearby are Amandine Bakeshop, Chopshop Café, and the Kurt Farm ice cream shop; they all call a one-time auto body shop home.

7. IT'S POST-AGRICULTURAL.

Same idea as post-industrial, only it's in a converted barn. For instance, Dill, the trend-setting Reykjavik restaurant, is coolly situated in a romantic and picturesque setting that once housed horses, cattle, and pigs. But if Iceland seems a little far to travel for such pastoral farmyard associations, Dill's Nordic chef Gunnar Gíslason is coming to New York to helm a restaurant in Grand Central Terminal—definitely *not* a barn.

8. IT SERVES HIGH-END FRENCH IN A STRIP MALL.

Petit Trois in LA has absolutely *nailed* this one. It's located in a funky strip mall, and what's outstanding about it is that they never took

down the signs of the two restaurants that were there before them: Tasty Thai and Raffallo's Pizza. Their garish yellow signs are still in place on the red aluminum tile roof. But below Tasty Thai, Cuisine of Thailand, is the charming front window of Petit Trois, which is framed in green and with elegant yellow lettering as if it were a little bistro on Boulevard San Michel rather than the corner of Highland and Melrose.

Petit Trois serves steak tartare, escargots a la Burgundy (the French-trained chef, Ludo Lefebvre, is Burgundian), confit-fried chicken leg, steak frites with Cognac pepper sauce, and, if you're in the mood, a double cheeseburger. This being LA, the place is lousy with Hollywood stars. Celebs, double cheese, French chef, strip mall—that's a certifiable viral explosion.

9. PEOPLE TALK FUNNY.

You know you're in the right place when the diners use terms like "food forward" and aren't embarrassed about it; they know what "M.O.F." means, and the goateed, tattooed chef de cuisine says things like, "The menu will feel more traditionally French than the food I cooked at Bones, but what is French food? Is it French product, or technique, or it is historical cooking?"

This was an actual, not made-up statement by Australian expat chef James Henry, commenting on the French or Not French food he was thinking about cooking for a Hong Kong restaurant he was opening. No one but a foodie talks like this, and only a foodie can understand it. Actually not even a foodie may know what Henry was saying.

10. IT APPEARED IN THE *FOODIE SNOB*.

This is so blatantly obvious we're almost embarrassed to mention it. But if we've written about something in this book, you know it's on fire and totally on trend. So don't hesitate. Post away!

THE SNOB 9

OLD-SCHOOL COOL: CLASSIC JOINTS THAT HAVE STOOD THE TEST OF TIME

It may be that you are on the prowl for the next Grant Achatz or Wylie Dufresne, in which case we say: Prowl on! When you find the Next Big Thing, post it on your Instagram feed and we'll be there.

Some nights, though, we're in the mood for something else—some old-school downtown restaurant cool, the kind of place Ryan Gosling would go if he were playing Dean Martin in a remake of *Matt Helm*. Here are ten of our favorite classic joints that are still relevant after all these years.

THE ODEON, NEW YORK
The heyday of The Odeon was the 1980s when the likes of Jerry Hall, Andy Warhol, John Belushi, Jack Nicholson, Jay McInerney (the sign in front appeared on the cover of his novel *Bright Lights, Big City*), and Julian Schnabel all ate and drank and partied there. Then things took a turn, not for the good. Belushi ODed, the drug scene got ugly, the artists left Tribeca and the bankers came in, 9/11 happened, there were recessions. It just wasn't as much fun as it was before.

But if you can survive the down days, and if you're lucky, a fickle public may rediscover you. That's what has happened with the O (the

insider's name for it). One World Trade Center has opened nearby. Literary and creative types have come back, as have the art and fashion crowds, all attracted by the restaurant's "dark corners" (writer Jacob Bernstein's evocative phrase) and the relative privacy of the spot. Regulars like publisher Judith Regan swear the food is better than it used to be at Elaine's, the gone-away Upper East Side literary hangout. TheOdeonRestaurant.com

THE MUSSO & FRANK GRILL, HOLLYWOOD

You expect an old-time Hollywood place to have lots of old-time Hollywood glamor, and this one does. It opened after World War I, and the stars who passed through these doors—Charlie Chaplin, Mary Pickford, Greta Garbo, Humphrey Bogart, Lauren Bacall, Jimmy Stewart, Marilyn Monroe—span from the silents to the Golden Age of Hollywood in the 1950s. Literary types like William Faulkner, Scott Fitzgerald, and Raymond Chandler also hung there, drinking mint juleps (Faulkner's favorite; he stepped behind the bar and made them himself) and dining on roast duck and French-cut lamb chops in a private room away from the prying eyes of the public.

The Back Room, as this room was called, is no more, but the worn leather booths and mahogany bar from those days remain intact. Try a martini; *GQ* and *Esquire* think it's one of the best they've had. MussoandFrank.com

SPAGO LAS VEGAS

Set the dial on the time-travel machine to 1991, Las Vegas. Now try to have a nice dinner on The Strip. Impossible, right? All you can find are buffets . . . buffets . . . and more buffets.

Enter Wolfgang Puck's Spago Las Vegas, which, like many old-time classic joints, was originally a trendsetter, ahead of its time. Featuring wood-fired oven pizzas and other aspects of Puck's creative

approach to California cuisine, Spago was hot stuff in Beverly Hills and swell places like that, but Vegas? Get real. People came to Vegas to gamble, maybe catch a show, but not to eat. When Spago opened in the Forum Shops Mall in Caesars Palace, people thought it was a joke, certain to fail.

Nobody's laughing now. As Larry Olmsted of *Forbes* has pointed out, Puck created a culinary revolution in Vegas, paving the way for just about every other celebrity chef in the world to open a restaurant there, turning it into a town where you can gamble, drink, party, see a show, *and* have a really nice meal. The patio extends out into the shopping mall like a sidewalk cafe, and it's great for people watching. WolfgangPuck.com

THE ROYAL HAWAIIAN, HONOLULU

This is one of the world's grandest hotel views. On the sands of Waikiki Beach, Diamond Head to your left, the turquoise waters of the Pacific Ocean stretching out to the horizon. Go ahead, have a mai tai; you earned it. BTW, Trader Vic Bergeron invented the mai tai, and the first one ever served in Hawaii was at the Pink Palace, as it's known for its surrealistic orangey-pink exterior.

After finishing one mai tai and moving on to your second, you will see in your mind's eye Natalie Wood or Bing Crosby or Dean Martin strolling by on the white sands; they all stayed here. Or maybe you can see Dean's buddy Frank Sinatra doing a scene from his Academy Award–winning role in *From Here to Eternity*, which featured the Palace. Another movie shot there was *Gidget Goes Hawaiian*. Miss that one? How about Adam Sandler's *Punch Drunk Love*?

On second thought, if you're beginning to see visions of Adam Sandler, it is time to stop drinking. Royal-Hawaiian.com

ANTOINE'S RESTAURANT, NEW ORLEANS

Open the dinner menu at Antoine's Restaurant and at the top of the list of appetizers you will see a listing for "*huitres en coquille* a la Rockefeller," and next to this, in parenthesis, it will say "*notre creation*." Translated, that means you can have a delicious serving of Louisiana gulf oysters baked on the half shell with the original Rockefeller sauce, which Antoine's created.

Antoine Alciatore founded this New Orleans restaurant before the Civil War, and his son Jules, a French-trained chef, invented the much-imitated oyster sauce, named after Rockefeller because of its richness. The relatives of Antoine and Jules still run the place, which is only a block or so from where the original stood. This is a grand Old World institution that seats up to seven hundred guests and has fourteen dining rooms, including the luxe Rex Room. One display features a Paris cookbook that predates Louis XIV. Antoines.com

TADICH GRILL, SAN FRANCISCO

Here's a three-sentence history of this venerable yet still vibrant San Francisco fish restaurant. They discovered gold in California. The next year Tadich Grill opened. It's been open ever since.

When you walk in, there's a long wooden bar that extends back to the kitchen. The bar stools are usually filled, as are the tables; it's a busy spot, especially at lunch. The tables have starched white tablecloths and the waiters wear white coats and ties like they're going to operate on you. On each table is a bowl of lemon quarters to squeeze onto the fish. House specialties are seafood cioppino with garlic bread, Australian lobster tail, and Hangtown Fry, which is oysters and bacon frittata. TadichGrill.com

UNION OYSTER HOUSE, BOSTON

Union Oyster House is one of those places that look and feel old, but in a good way. US Senator Daniel Webster dined on brandy and oysters there in the 1850s. It is said that a lumber family in Maine invented the toothpick, and the first time anyone ever used one at a commercial establishment was here.

Ordinarily we might be skeptical of a story like that, but there are so many true stories about the Oyster House, we're inclined to believe that one too. True story: President Jack Kennedy ate there regularly on Sunday when he was in Boston (he loved the lobster stew). Also true: Luciano Pavarotti was having lunch when he overheard the group sitting in the booth next to him celebrating a birthday. He stood up and sang them "Happy Birthday."

It's a block from Faneuil Hall. The oyster bars and stalls are located in the same position they were in 1826, the year the Oyster House opened. On the menu: Cherrystone, Littleneck, and other oysters; mussels; fish chowder; clam chowder; and, yes, Boston baked beans. UnionOysterHouse.com

THE BERGHOFF, CHICAGO

The Berghoff is a story of America all by itself. The founder, Herman Berghoff, immigrated to this country from Germany as a teen. He started a brewery in Indiana and, then, looking for a way to sell the beer he was making, founded a saloon in downtown Chicago near the Loop. When it opened in 1898, only men could drink there. They served corned beef sandwiches, which were free as long as you bought a glass or stein of Berghoff beer, five and ten cents respectively.

Then came the dark dry days of Prohibition, and the Berghoff had to change to stay alive. It morphed into a restaurant for reliably hearty

German food. Then it obtained the first post-Prohibition liquor license issued by the city of Chicago. The restaurant, serving food *and* drink, is where to go; it has black-and-white photos of old Chicago on the walls and offers Wiener schnitzel, sauerbraten, and German gnocchi. TheBerghoff.com

VERSAILLES, MIAMI

The name sounds French, and the retro architecture and decor trend that way too, but Versailles (pronounced "ver-say-ez") is as old-school Cuban as Desi Arnaz or Xavier Cugat. Feeling adventurous? Try the Wednesday special: pigs' feet Andalusian style. No? Go classic then: *Ropa vieja*, which means "old clothes" in Spanish; it's stuffed green plantains. Or hell, why not, you're in Little Havana: the Cuban sandwich.

The unofficial city hall of Little Havana, where political deals are hatched and consummated, Versailles stays open till two in the morning on weekdays and four in the morning on Friday and Saturday nights, which makes it, in blogger Priscilla Blossom's words, "the Jersey diner of Little Havana. Grab a café cubano, a guava pastellito and have a seat." Great idea. VersaillesRestaurant.com

FOODIE SNOB QUIZ #5

FOOD MOVIES

Of all the quizzes in this book, this one could easily have one hundred questions and still not exhaust the subject. There are many fine movies with food themes; then there are all the movies in which food figures into a scene or scenes. It's *a lot.*

We had to keep the list to ten questions, however. Answers are hidden in plain sight in their usual place.

1. To show off his cooking cred and introduce him to the audience at the start of *Ratatouille,* Chef Auguste Gusteau appears on the cover of several food magazines. Which of these magazines did he NOT appear on?
   a. *Food and Wine*
   b. *Bon Appetit*
   c. *Gourmet*
   d. *Cook's Illustrated*
2. Alice Waters has loved the movies of this French actor-filmmaker since she was a young woman. His movie posters adorn the walls of Chez Panisse and even the name *Panisse* is a character in his films. His name, *s'l vous plait.*
   a. Maurice Chevalier
   b. Jean Paul Belmondo

c. Marcel Pagnol

d. Francois Truffaut

3. In *Babette's Feast*, the wondrous Danish film, a French servant named Babette prepares a beautiful meal for two religiously devout sisters and their friends, serving blinis Demidoff with caviar, *Cailles en Sarcophage*, Veuve Clicquot, and other French pleasures they had never tasted before. The sisters, though kind-hearted, were terrible cooks. What foul-tasting dish did they like to serve people?

   a. pickled herring

   b. ale soup

   c. boiled cabbage

   d. brains and eggs

4. In the opening scene of *The Big Night*, Secondo (Stanley Tucci) and Primo (Tony Shaloub) have a disagreement with an unpleasant female diner who insists on having a side dish with her risotto. What dish do they eventually serve this—to quote Primo—"Philistine"?

   a. pizza

   b. ravioli

   c. spaghetti and meatballs

   d. linguine with clam sauce

5. Anthony Hopkins as Hannibal Lecter uttered one of the most memorable food lines in movie history in *The Silence of the Lambs*. Talking to Agent Starling (Jodie Foster) from his cell, he warns her that he once ate a man's liver "with some fava beans and a nice Chianti." What did his victim do?

   a. food blogger

   b. tax preparer

   c. census taker

   d. attorney

6. Tita is the heroine of *Like Water for Chocolate*, a Mexican romance about food and star-crossed love. Early in the film she cooks a meal so seductive and delicious it causes her sister to tear off her clothes, run away with a horseman, and join the revolution. What was the dish?

   a. quail in rose petal sauce

   b. chile rellenos with roasted peppers and walnuts

   c. *mole*

   d. enchiladas

7. British actors Steve Coogan and Rob Brydon starred in two entertaining food and travel comedies, *The Trip* and *The Trip to Italy*. In one of their best bits they do impersonations of the British actor who appeared as Batman's butler and co-owns Langan's Brasserie in London. Name the actor.

   a. Sean Connery

   b. Hugh Grant

   c. Michael Caine

   d. Sir John Gielgud

8. Nora Ephron's love for men and good food (not necessarily in that order) comes through in her screenplays for *When Harry Met Sally*, *Heartburn*, and *Julie & Julia*. The funniest and most memorable food scene she wrote was in *When Harry Met Sally* when Meg Ryan demonstrated a fake orgasm to Billy Crystal while they were eating lunch at a landmark New York deli. What was the deli?

   a. Carnegie Deli

   b. Zabar's

   c. Russ & Daughters

   d. Katz's

9. It's a little-known fact that Jiro Ono, the stellar Japanese sushi chef (and the star of the fascinating documentary *Jiro Dreams of Sushi*) served as the inspiration for Mr. Miyagi, the character played by Pat Morita in the original *Karate Kid*. Ono, a ten-degree black belt when he was young (the highest level), also advised on the film, particularly the key scene where Miyagi counsels the Kid to land lightly on the ground after a kick as if touching a grape.

Question: Is the preceding statement true or false?

10. Roy Choi advised on Jon Favreau's *Chef* and appeared at the end of the closing credits giving the actor-director-writer a cooking lesson. What was Choi teaching Favreau how to make?

   a. Korean BBQ taco
   b. grilled cheese sandwich
   c. bibimbap
   d. chicken Caesar salad

Answers: 1. d; 2. c; 3. b; 4. c; 5. c; 6. b; 7. c; 8. d; 9 False (Ono did star in the documentary, but there is no connection between him and Mr. Miyagi.); 10. b

Answer to the Match Game: Star Chefs and Mentors on page 155. The secret code is that the chef on the left is listed in every case directly across from his or her mentor on the right. Batali's mentor was Tower, Achatz's was Keller, Garten's was Stewart, and so on.

CHAPTER SIX

Adventures in food

There is food tourism; and there are food adventures. We prefer the latter. But what defines a food adventure, and how do you go about having one? You can dig deep into the cuisine of a foreign country or seek "peak dining experiences" in far-flung places abroad. There is a lot to discover here at home too; you can find unexpectedly good food at a highway stand on a weekend road trip. Or you can even delve into the past, looking into your family's food and cooking history and following that inspiration wherever it leads. The world, as some foodie said once, is your oyster, and in the next pages we'll travel down some twisty paths in quest of food adventures.

THE IMPORTANCE OF MOLE

RICK BAYLESS SHOWS US HOW TO GO DEEP

Mole is the national dish of Mexico, and yet many Americans, even ones who love Mexican food, have never tasted it. They would rather have tacos and enchiladas, which are delicious when prepared well, yet there is so much more to Mexican cuisine than that.

This is Rick Bayless's core message. He's the well-known TV personality, cookbook author, and chef-owner of two Mexican restaurants in Chicago: Frontera Grill and Topolobampo. When he was young and finding his way as a chef, Bayless dug deep into Mexican cuisine and got to know it in a way few gringos do, and one of the things he found out about was *mole.* Here are four basic lessons he learned.

YOU CAN GET BAD *MOLE* EVEN IN MEXICO.
This was a key discovery for Bayless, and one that every food enthusiast looking to explore the cuisine of a foreign country ought to keep in mind. Yes, *mole* is the national dish, but that doesn't mean everyone in Mexico knows how to cook it well. Furthermore, even if a chef knows how to make an authentic version of *mole*, he may not

serve it that way to his customers. This is particularly true for the tourist restaurants in the big cities.

"It is unfortunate," says Bayless, "that most people's first experience with *mole* is usually in a tourist-oriented restaurant in Mexico." These restaurants tend to use commercially prepared pastes, cook with too much oil, and overly sweeten the dish, he says. Understandably perhaps, they prepare it in such a way as to please the palates of the many American tourists who eat there. The result, however, is not good.

KNOWING SPANISH, AT LEAST A LITTLE, CAN DEEPEN YOUR APPRECIATION OF *MOLE*.

It would seem, if you are one of those American tourists, you have done everything right. You have come to Mexico City and sought out a prominent restaurant, one recommended by a guidebook. And you have spent more than a few pesos to do this. And yet, after all that, you're still not tasting the real thing. What is a person supposed to do?

Dig a little deeper, says Bayless.

People learn to "talk menu" when they travel, familiarizing themselves with Spanish or French or Italian just enough so they can read (mostly) what's on a menu and perhaps speak to a waiter and understand some of what he is saying. Of course, many restaurant people in Mexico and around the world speak English, but in Bayless's view, if you play it safe and stick only to your own language, that fully realized gastronomic experience you're seeking will not be as full or as realized as it could be. You're going to miss a lot.

"So what, then, is a *mole*?" writes Bayless whose cookbooks contain lessons in etymology as well as food. "Looking at the history of the

word shines a little light on the subject. *Mole* is the hispanization of a Nahuatl word (*molli*) that means 'sauce.'" Nahuatl was the language of the Aztecs, which suggests that the origins of the sauce date from well before the birth of Mexico as a country. There are more than a million people of Aztec descent who speak Nahuatl in Mexico today.

HAVING A *MOLE* IS A GEOGRAPHY LESSON.

Just like the United States or Canada, Mexico is not one big lumpy amorphous mass of a country; it has distinct regions or states, and each region has its own identity, its own way of doing things, its own cuisine. The best-known *mole* region is the coastal state of Guerrero, home of Acapulco. They make a red *mole* there—*Guajalote en mole Teloloapense*, which Bayless learned to make when he was living in Guerrero and roaming the fruit and vegetable markets in the mountains of Tixtla looking for fresh ingredients to cook with.

As evidenced by the amount of time it takes to make certain *moles* (the greater part of a day or spread out over a few days), it is a dish for fiestas and special occasions in Mexico, and you will find it on most every restaurant menu. Another region that prides itself on its *moles* is Oaxaca, on Guerrero's southern border and also a land of beaches and mountains. But even here, two thousand miles south

of San Diego, one must be wary of not getting the real thing. At the touristy *zócalo* (central square) cafes, you can be served another of those overly sweetened *moles* that are so black they look like dried tar. Search out instead Abigail Mendoza's interpretation of *mole* at her Tlamanalli restaurant in Teotitlan del Valle. "Her version is what dreams are made of," reports Bayless.

YOU DON'T HAVE TO BE MEXICAN TO COOK AUTHENTIC MEXICAN FOOD AND LOVE IT.

This is a frequent theme of Bayless; he refers to it all the time. "Can a gringo guy with popular Stateside restaurants flesh out the nuances of Mexico's real cooking?" he asks, although he is a living embodiment of the answer.

He is from Oklahoma City. His parents owned and operated a Hickory House barbecue restaurant in town. After church the family would get together for Sunday supper and eat fried chicken and peach cobbler with vanilla ice cream. After discovering the country to his south and getting hooked on its cuisine, he evolved into what he describes as a kind of culinary translator, making authentic Mexican food that his countrymen can relate to.

This can act as both inspiration and moral of the story. You can be a gringo and cook Mexican. You can eat Dinty Moore out of a can as a boy and become a Michelin three-star French chef. You can be born in Ethiopia and learn to cook Swedish and make American-style Southern fried chicken. You can be a movie star and turn your homemade salad dressing recipe into a business that raises millions for charity. You can be an American woman of a certain age, not know how to boil water, then attend a snobby French cooking school dominated by men and lead a food revolution in your country. Sometimes all it takes is a willingness to go deep.

SNOB ADVICE

When you're going deep into Mexican food, don't forget Diana Kennedy. Well before Rick Bayless appeared on the scene, she pioneered authentic Mexican cooking for gringo (she's a Brit) audiences. She eventually made her home in Michoacán, another food-rich state in Mexico. Her books, including updated versions of *The Essential Cuisines of Mexico* and *The Art of Mexican Cooking*, are classics of the genre.

NOT AS MYSTERIOUS AS ALL THAT

MARTIN YAN POINTS OUT 5 MISCONCEPTIONS ABOUT CHINATOWNS AND CHINESE FOOD

Much like Rick Bayless, Martin Yan sees himself as a translator or popularizer—"a cultural bridge to Chinese cuisine," as he describes it. In his television programs and books, he takes food enthusiasts into places they have never been before; or they may have been there but only briefly and superficially and they do not understand it as well as they would like.

Places like Chinatown. Long a metaphor in mainstream culture for an exotic, slightly sinister otherworld of mystery and intrigue—see Roman Polanski's *Chinatown*, starring Jack Nicholson, if you doubt this—the Chinatowns that Martin Yan knows are nothing like this. While building bridges he has also done major demolition work on popular misconceptions about Chinatown and Chinese food. Here are five of those misconceptions.

1. EVERY CHINATOWN IS THE SAME.

Yan, who was born in Guangzhou (Canton), China, never lived in a Chinatown. His widowed mother, fearing that she could not provide for her son and seeing how limited his opportunities were at home, sent him away at the age of thirteen to an uncle who lived in Hong Kong. There he entered into his first formal training in cooking before eventually migrating to Canada and the United States.

Once he broke into television and became a brand-name chef—you gotta have an angle, as they say, and Yan became famous for being able to debone a chicken in eighteen seconds—one of his most personally rewarding projects was to travel to various Chinatowns around the world to learn about the food, culture, and people. What surprised him the most was how different they are. From the former Portugese colony of Macau to Singapore (home of "the world's best and most expensive fried rice"), from Sydney and London to Vancouver (aka "Van Kong," for its large and growing Chinese immigrant population), and New York and San Francisco, "there was never the monolithic Chinatown," he explains. Chinese immigrants are like other immigrants most everywhere: While they remain linked in various ways to their native countries, they adapt to the customs and norms of their new home.

2. SINCE HE'S CHINESE, HE KNOWS EVERYTHING THERE IS TO KNOW ABOUT CHINESE FOOD INSTINCTIVELY.

Yan learned to cook in his mother's kitchen. Then, after moving to Hong Kong to stay with his uncle, he managed to enroll as a teenager in a prestigious cooking school there. Flat broke and with his uncle unable to pay his tuition, he did this by striking a bargain with the school's owner. The owner said that if the boy shopped for ingredients at the street markets every day and carried everything up to the school before class started, Yan would not have to pay tuition. So he did, rising every morning before sunup, getting what the students needed to cook with that day, and carrying all of it to the school. They held classes on the seventh floor of a walkup building.

Here is the secret of how Yan learned Chinese cooking—and it's similar to how Bayless learned Mexican. He studied, he worked hard, he cooked, he tasted, he kept his mind open. One constant was his desire to learn and better himself.

SNOB ASIDE

Feeling adventurous? The Chinese say they have more than one hundred ways to prepare an egg. One of them is the century egg (or hundred-year-old egg or thousand-year-old egg); it's a duck egg steeped in salt over weeks or months, and traditional methods call for the preservation to be done without refrigeration. If that's not exotic enough for you, try some steamed worms or chop up live insects and fish before cooking them. The Chinese do that too.

3. AMERICANS ARE NOT VERY ADVENTUROUS WHEN IT COMES TO CHINESE FOOD.

Yan immigrated first to Canada before journeying down to the Lower 48 to study food science at the University of California at Davis,

where he graduated. In time he went back to Canada to help a friend open a Chinese restaurant in Alberta province, and this was where his big break occurred. A local television producer saw him doing a cooking demo at a restaurant and invited him to be a guest on a talk program. His likeability and ease on the air led to his own show and thousands of television appearances later, he seems to have developed a knack for it.

When Yan started cooking on television in the 1970s, basically he made chop suey and chow mein for North American audiences who knew little about Chinese food and weren't all that curious about it. That has steadily changed over the years, and once-exotic dishes such as Kung Pao chicken, General Tso chicken, sweet-and-sour chicken, and moo shu pork have become popular standards. And things are opening up still more, Yan says approvingly. While many still do play it safe with the time-honored standards, younger diners tend to be "more curious, articulate and adventurous. They're more willing to accept new cuisines and ingredients."

4. CHINESE FOOD IS THE SAME EVERYWHERE.

One lingering misconception about so-called ethnic food is that within a certain cuisine, it's all the same; Chinese is Chinese, Mexican is Mexican, Indian is Indian, Thai is Thai. This is plainly silly, like saying the regional cuisines of Austin, New Orleans, and Bangor, Maine, are identical.

Being the most populous country on Earth, China has multiple regions that differ widely, and these differences show up in what people eat and how they prepare it. There is Yan's home region of Canton; Sichuan and Hunan in the west; Shanghai and Fuzhou in the east; Beijing in the north. Each uses somewhat different techniques

and different ingredients to make a dish, and there are endless examples of this. One is dim sum, which originated in Canton and traditionally is filled with ground meat. But in Shanghai the center of a *siu mai* dumpling is sticky rice.

5. THERE IS ONLY ONE FILLING FOR *JUNG*.

One of the ironies noted by Yan in his travels is that he had to leave China and come to America in order to fully appreciate Chinese food. As a boy growing up in Guangzhou, he loved eating *jung*, a leaf-wrapped rice dumpling. But even then he noticed they only made it one way in Guangzhou, the traditional way. Years later when he came to San Francisco—the site of his favorite Chinatown, by the way—the bonds of tradition had been loosened, and people were making *jung* in far different ways than they had back home.

The San Francisco Bay Area is now Yan's home. It is where he celebrates the Chinese New Year, Dragon Boat Festival, and other Chinese ceremonies, and where he eats a gorgeous variety of *jungs* filled with cherries, berries, peaches, lotus seed, date pastes, pork, chicken, dried shrimp, mushrooms, and other centers. "Sometimes," he reflects, "you have to leave home and roam the world before you learn to appreciate the heritage and resources in your own backyard."

TRUMAN CAPOTE AND THE FRUITCAKE LADY

WITH CAMEO APPEARANCES BY JAY LENO, MEL GIBSON, AND TOM CRUISE

Here's another food truism: Not only are there regional cuisines within a larger national cuisine, there are different cuisines within a single region, such as in the American South.

There is the French- and Caribbean-inspired Creole cuisine of Louisiana Bayou country, the spicy Latin and Cuban flavors of Little Havana, and traditional Southern food such as fried chicken, mashed taters, grits, and black-eyed peas. Stretching the regional boundaries a bit, one might even include Tex-Mex fare from the Southwest.

And if you would really like to travel into the Deep South, gastronomically speaking, have a piece of Aunt Phronie's pumpkin pie or some Tallahassee hush puppies, compliments of the hand-me-down recipes of Sook Faulk of Monroeville, Alabama. Some of Faulk's collected recipes date from the plantation days before the Civil War.

Sook Faulk died a long time ago, and the reason we still have her old, old, old recipes is a story worth telling. Her niece, also an Alabaman, was a woman named Marie Rudisill, and if that name doesn't ring a bell maybe this one will: the Fruitcake Lady. Rudisill, aka the Fruitcake Lady, became a minor television celebrity by appearing on Jay Leno's *The Tonight Show* in the early 2000s when she was in her nineties and nearing the end of her life. She did some cooking demos on the show with Jay, making a fruitcake with Mel Gibson and a cherry pie with Cuba Gooding Jr. But her most popular bit was a repeating segment on the show, "Ask the Fruitcake Lady," in which she answered random questions from viewers in a crotchety yet amusing old lady way.

How this all came about was that Leno was making jokes about fruitcakes in his monologue—a long comic tradition; see Calvin Trillin or Leno's *Tonight Show* predecessor Johnny Carson—and Rudisill wrote him a letter in protest, saying they deserved more respect. This stirred the interest of a producer; they put her on the show, and she was a hit. "Do you think Santa will bring me a rich man who loves to cook and clean around the house?" a woman asked her one night during the "Ask the Fruitcake Lady" segment. "No," she snapped. "Of course not, because there is no such man on earth. No such man."

Her silver hair tied back in an attractive bun, Rudisill had a soft Alabama twang that made her blunt opinions that much more endearing. She had lived life too; that gave her authority, and she knew Southern food. Although she published a few books after becoming a Tonight Show celebrity, her best book, *Sook's Cookbook*, came out before she ever went on the show. It was a collection of "receipts," as she called them, using the traditional term that her aunt Sook Faulk had passed down to her before she died. "The understanding was," Rudisill explained, "that I would share them with Truman Capote, my

sister's child, who had been brought up in Sook's hometown of Monroeville, Alabama."

Capote, the writer and journalist, lived in Monroeville as a boy. So did his friend Harper Lee and Rudisill, of course. His closest friend in the world, though, was his distant cousin, Sook Faulk, who appears in a leading role in Capote's story "A Christmas Memory," easily the finest example of fruitcake literature in the American canon; although, we concede, it is not a vast canon. In it he recalls making fruitcakes with Sook ("It's fruitcake weather," she says, to begin their cooking quest), gathering and hulling the pecans, buying the whiskey, cherries, citron, canned Hawaiian pineapple, and other ingredients with the pennies they had saved in "the Fruitcake Fund," and then cooking it all up over four days in the kitchen.

"The black stove, stoked with coal and firewood, glows like a lighted pumpkin," Capote writes. "Eggbeaters whirl, spoons spin round in bowls of butter and sugar, vanilla sweetens the air, ginger spices it; melting, nose-tingling odors saturate the kitchen, suffuse the house, drift out to the world on puffs of chimney smoke. Thirty-one cakes, dampened with whiskey, bask on window sills and shelves."

"The Thanksgiving Visitor" is another Capote story that features Sook Faulk and loving accounts of her holiday meal-making as well as a dramatic family gathering in which Buddy, who is Capote as a boy, plays a mean trick on another boy, a guest on Thanksgiving. Afterward Sook schools Buddy on why the trick he played was so wrong: "What you did was much worse: you planned to humiliate him. It was deliberate. Now listen to me, Buddy: there is only one unpardonable sin—*deliberate cruelty*. All else can be forgiven. That, never. Do you understand me, Buddy?"

Capote never forgot Sook and never forgot that lesson. Rudisill's collection of family receipts is beautifully illustrated by Barry Moser and for five minutes of viewing pleasure, search the Fruitcake Lady and Jay Leno on YouTube to watch Marie make a fruitcake with Tom Cruise; it's a sweet treat.

VINTAGE SOUL

Soul Food, written and directed by George Tillman Jr., is an underappreciated film about the joys and travails of family life and how the dinner table can act as a safe space for families to come together despite ongoing tension and friction. "People always said she never had an enemy in her life," says the boy in the movie who acts as narrator, describing his grandmother Big Mama, "because if she did she'd have 'em over for her green beans, sweet potato pie, and Southern fried chicken."

Big Mama's death splits the family apart, but there's never a disagreement about the food they like. We see them making and serving and loving on ham hocks, pig's feet, chitlins, black-eyed peas, egg pie, macaroni and cheese, lima beans, neck bones, collard greens with hot sauce, hot cakes, cornbread, dumplings, deep-fried catfish, corn on the cob, and fried chicken. The biggest eater in the group is Reverend Williams, who comes over to the house after church to share Sunday supper with them.

The family migrated to Chicago from the South, but they brought their love of soul food with them, and the boy explains why it means so much to them: "See, during slavery us blacks didn't have a whole lot to celebrate. Cooking became our way of how we expressed our love for each other. That's what those Sunday dinners meant to us. More than just eating, it was a time to share our joys and sorrows, something the old folks say is missing these days." Vanessa Williams and Vivica A. Fox star.

LITTLE FOODIE HOUSE
ON THE PRAIRIE

Another piece of Americana full of food is Laura Ingalls Wilder's *Little House on the Prairie*. Yes, it's a children's novel written eons ago, but the storytelling is first rate and it is impossible not to appreciate the irony of how one of today's hottest food trends, cooking over an open fire a la Francis Mallmann in the Pampas, was done routinely by Indians and settlers crossing the West centuries ago.

When she was a girl, Ingalls Wilder's family left Wisconsin to homestead on the Great Plains in the late 1800s. They traveled by Conestoga wagon, and on a lunch break "they sat on the clean grass and ate pancakes and bacon and molasses from the tin plates on their laps." When they finally reached their destination near the Verdigris River in Kansas, her father cleared the land; cut the trees; built the house, chimney, and fireplace where they cooked their meals; and built the table where they ate them. He built the chairs too.

It was all DIY back then, including for Ma who made the cornbread from scratch. "Ma rolled up her sleeves and washed her hands and mixed cornbread. Ma made the cornmeal and water into two thin loaves, each shaped in a half

circle. She laid the loaves with their straight sides together in the bake-oven, and she pressed her hand flat on top of each loaf."

She cooked the wild game that Pa shot, and for Christmas dinner one year they had a "tender, juicy, roasted turkey. There were the sweet potatoes, baked in the ashes and carefully wiped so that you could eat the good skins, too. There was a loaf of salt-rising bread made from the last of the white flour."

Store-bought items such as salt, salt pork, cornmeal, and coffee were hard to come by, seeing that the closest store was in Independence two days away. White sugar was a rare delicacy. In their stockings that Christmas, Laura and her sister each received a new tin cup, a stick of peppermint candy, and a mysterious package. "They unwrapped them, and each found a little heart-shaped cake. Over their delicate brown tops was sprinkled white sugar. The sparkling grains lay like tiny drifts of snow."

Little House on the Prairie came second in the series; first was *Little House in the Big Woods*. It too has marvelous food writing. Melissa Gilbert, star of the old television program based on Little

House, wrote a cookbook inspired by the show and plains-style cooking. In Cara Nicoletti's cookbook *Voracious*, she develops recipes and makes meals based on the ones described in classics of literature such as *In Cold Blood*, *To Kill a Mockingbird*, and *Moby Dick*. Her Laura Ingalls Wilder recipe was breakfast sausage with ground pork shoulder, sage, and maple syrup.

ROADSIDE FINDS

8 WAYS TO KNOW YOU'VE FOUND A PLACE THAT'S TRULY SPECIAL

Craig Claiborne called them "roadside finds"—a somewhat antiquated term for one of the real pleasures of being a foodie: discovering a truly good and authentic place that no one (no one who matters, that is) has heard of.

But with all these food bloggers and TV hosts roaming the globe in perpetual search for "The Next Big Thing," it's getting harder and harder to uncover a true roadside find. Here are eight ways to tell if the place you've alighted upon is truly unique.

1. YOU'VE NEVER SEEN IT ON TV.

If the menu says, "As Seen on Guy Fieri!" or if the *Day of Gluttony* guys have swept through or God forbid, Rick Steves has come by

and nursed a glass of Chardonnay there, forget it. You're too late; move on.

2. ONLY LOCALS ARE THERE.

When you step in the door, do a fast visual assessment of the clientele. If nobody is there taking pictures of their food or tweeting about it or in deep discussion about the spices in a unique avocado dipping sauce—in other words, *if there is nobody in the place like you*—it's safe to go in. This could be the real thing.

3. IT'S A LITTLE BIT FUNKY.

You *can* make restaurant discoveries in places with white tablecloths and polished silverware, but typically not. For example, one of food critic Bryan Miller's favorite roadside finds is a crawfish restaurant in the boonies of southwest Louisiana called Hawk's. Hawk's is a locals' place, there are lots of old guys in Stetsons and Wrangler shirts with snap-button pockets, and it's in a ramshackle former barn with a big painting of a red crawfish on the front door. Above the door it says, "Home of The Best Boiled Crawfish in the World." That's just about right.

4. IT'S AT THE END OF A LONG, LONG, LONG, LONG, LONG ROAD.

Hawk's is like that; so is Magnus Nilsson's Faviken located somewhere deep in the Swedish tundra. You lost cell coverage an hour ago, and you're still not there. You know it has to be good, because nobody actually knows where it is. Ask around. Has anyone you know ever eaten there? Faviken may be urban folklore; it may not even exist. In any case, if you're hiring a dog sled to go have dinner, it's probably a pretty awesome place.

5. THE FOOD IS EXOTIC.

The TV guys are all over this one. Anthony Bourdain once ate balut—fetal duck egg—in Vietnam and lived to tell about it. That's key; choking and dying after a meal tends to depress ratings. In Sardinia the *Bizarre Foods* guy, Andrew Zimmern, dined on *casu marzu*, which is cheese with live maggots in it. It's illegal to sell, but the Sardinians still make it and serve it, at least to visiting TV hosts in need of a novel story angle. But it is true that if you're going to go way, way out there in search of eats, you can't just have ham and eggs—unless, perhaps, the ham is *jamón Ibérico* cured by an ancient Basque farmer whose family has been doing it for generations.

6. THE CHEF IS A DEEP, DEEP THINKER.

Virtually all the guys and gals profiled on the Netflix series *The Chef's Table* qualify on this score. For instance, Francis Mallman says guru-type things like, "My life has been a path at the edge of uncertainty" and "I think that the worst enemies we have in life are routine and fear. They are the two things that paralyze us." Like all good chef-gurus, the charismatic Mallman is primal, earthy, cosmic—and his country home is at the end of a long, long, long road in the wilds of Patagonia.

7. THE RESTAURANT MAKES IT HARD FOR YOU TO FIND IT.

Grant Achatz of Alinea is another of the deep-thinking *Chef's Table* chefs, so deep, in fact, he dislikes having to serve his avant-garde creations on conventional plates and bowls. "It frustrated me," he said on the program, "that as chefs we were limited to scale that was determined by plate manufacturers. Why not a tablecloth that we can eat off of? Why do you have to eat with a fork or a spoon? Why do we have to serve in a bowl?"

Achatz is rethinking the dining experience from the ground up, including making it hard for guests to find where they're actually supposed to eat. The dining room is off a hallway, and it is not immediately clear how to reach it after you enter the building. And if a guest should somehow get lost on his way to the dining room? "I don't even want to tell them how to get into the place," says one of Achatz's kitchen lieutenants.

Actually, Tokyo restaurants, which are legendarily hard to locate, have been working this angle for years. If you can't find the place, that's where you want to be.

8. IT'S CLOSED PART OF THE YEAR.

Ferran Adria wrote the playbook on this one, as El Bulli was open only six months of the year (and not for lunch). Although one would never describe what was once the world's greatest restaurant in such an offhand manner, El Bulli nevertheless possessed several of the key characteristics of a classic roadside find: remote Spanish location, down a long and winding road, chef-guru, exotic fare. But it's long been shuttered, so if you're in quest of the new El Bulli or Hawk's, you'll have to find your own.

Footnote: Ferran has joined with his brother Albert to form a new restaurant/gastronomic experience in Barcelona, which, according to its website, is "the most exciting, complex, sophisticated and imaginative project *of all time*." (Emphasis added.) This may be another quality to look for in a roadside find: modesty.

THE SNOB 7

PEAK DINING EXPERIENCES, CONTINENT BY CONTINENT

In mountain climbing, it is the Seven Sacred Summits, the highest peaks on seven continents: Everest, Aconcagua, McKinley, Kilimanjaro, Elbrus, Vinson Massif, Carstensz Pyramid.

In long distance running, it is the World Marathon Majors, the top six marathon races in the world: Boston, New York, Chicago, London, Berlin, Tokyo.

But there has been no fine dining equivalent of the Seven Sacred Summits or the World Marathon Majors—until now. Here is our list of seven peak dining experiences, all extraordinary and amazing gastronomic adventures for the food traveler.

This is our one and only inviolable rule: One ultimate gastronomic experience per continent. As unfair and arbitrary as this is, it is nonetheless the rule. There are lots of mountains in the Himalayas that are taller than McKinley or Kilimanjaro, but only the tallest Himalayan peak, Mount Everest, makes it onto the list of the Seven Summits. McKinley and Kilimanjaro represent their continents, North America and Africa.

This rule has the added benefit of making this a truly global list, unlike the World Marathon Majors, which seems tilted toward the

United States and Europe. The world of food is, truly, a world, and so our choices for peak dining experiences reflect that. Let the arguments begin.

ANTARCTICA: CONCORDIA STATION

Easily the best place to sit down for a meal in Antarctica, the southernmost continent, is Concordia Station. Situated in one of the coldest and driest places on Earth, Concordia is 12,500 feet high and so isolated that people can only go in and out of it three months of the year in summer. It's a research base operated jointly by France and Italy.

Given the culinary traditions of the two host countries, it is no surprise that Concordia is *the* top ticket in Antarctica fine dining (and the only one, to be honest). Multicourse gourmet lunches and dinners are served, with imported wines, and the chef uses fresh ingredients until they run out, at which point he goes to the larder for the canned and frozen provisions. The chef changes from year to year, so it is hard to know what to recommend. Past chef Giorgio Deidda, an Italian, made what was said to be scrumptious pasta based on his mother's recipes, and team members raved about the work of another chef, Sicilian Luca Ficara, and his seafood pastry lattice with scallops, prawns, and fresh French cream.

Since only scientists and research team members can go to Concordia—no tourists—we must suggest, albeit reluctantly, a nearby dining alternative: the Woodbine Café in the Falkland Islands.

The Falklands (or Islas Malvinas, if you swing that way) is a stopover for cruise ships headed to the South Pole, and the Woodbine is where everybody goes when they're in port. It's been there for decades, some Brits run it, and it delivers, in the words of a Falklander, "reliably tasty fish and chips." While fish-and-chips may not be anyone's defi-

nition of a peak dining experience, when you've been eating cruise ship food for that long and come that far, it probably does taste pretty good. For fish they use mullet caught in local waters, deep-sea grenadiers, and imported haddock.

SOUTH AMERICA: D.O.M., SAO PAULO, BRAZIL

One of the characteristics of a peak dining experience is that it cannot be presented to you on a silver platter, as it were; it must be relatively inaccessible, hard to get to, off the beaten track. So it is with D.O.M. in Sao Paulo, an urban jungle south of the glam beaches of Rio de Janeiro and a couple of hours inland from the ocean. *The Lonely Planet* describes the city, without hyperbole, as "a monster. Enormous, intimidating and at first glance, no great beauty." But like every city Sao Paulo offers beautiful treasures if you're open to them, and one of those treasures is Alex Atala's D.O.M.

What is so intriguing about D.O.M and its famous chef Alex Atala—he has won two Michelin stars, the first chef of a South American restaurant to do so, and has been blessed by Ferran Adria and profiled by Netflix—is that they present the opportunity to taste different flavors, *very* different flavors, culled from and inspired by the horn of plenty that is the Amazon. Some of the biggest freshwater fish in the world are found in the rain forests of the Amazon, not to mention an exotic array of herbs, edible flowers, and buds. A Brazilian national hero for raising the reputation of the country's cuisine, Atala makes dishes— Tucupi sauce, the priprioca root, Paraiba Valley black rice, palmetto pupunhaand—whose ingredients are found only in the Amazon.

The tasting menu includes Amazon ants, a favorite food of the indigenous Baniwa tribe. Ants are served in a variety of ways, including one perched atop a small cube of pineapple. You eat the ant and the pineapple with your fingers. DOMRestaurante.com.br

AUSTRALIA: SEPIA, SYDNEY

Rules were made to be broken, and we broke them all to name Sepia Restaurant and Wine Bar as our peak dining experience for the Land Down Under. It's in Darling Park in Sydney, which (once you're in Australia, of course) is a snap to get to; it's steps away from the Darling Harbor waterfront with its aquarium and maritime museum and a quick ten-minute cab ride to the Opera House. The chef is Martin Benn, who trained under the Australian-born Japanese chef Tetsuya Wakuda—which is fitting, because Benn's silken cuttlefish and other intensely flavored fish dishes are Japanese inspired, though Benn himself is English-born and French-trained. Eric Ripert, who's a pretty international cat himself, has called it one of the top-five restaurants in the world.

The nine-course menu begins with a tasting of saikou salmon, smoked scarlet prawn, and Hiramasa kingfish and includes charcoal-grilled abalone and roasted Aylesbury duck breast. An added bonus: Sepia is suave, sophisticated, a place for putting on the Ritz. The smoky hot introduction to its website is the best online restaurant film we've seen. SepiaRestaurant.com.au

SNOB ASIDE

The best restaurant city in the world? Ask David Chang of Momofuku and it's no contest: Tokyo. Here are a few of his reasons: more Michelin stars than any other city in the world; the best sushi anywhere *and* the best steakhouses; the freshest fish, which moves daily through the Tsukiji Market; fewer restrictive food importation laws. Hell, in Chang's view, it even has the best *airport* food. Says he: "Japan as a country is devoted to food, and in Tokyo that fixation is exponentially multiplied. It's a city of places built on top of each other, a mass complex of restaurants."

ASIA: ISHIKAWA, TOKYO

In the mass complex of restaurants that is Tokyo, is Ishikawa the best of the best? We would never make such a claim. It is, however, a Michelin three-star restaurant, and David Kinch, a Michelin three-star chef himself (Manresa in Los Gatos, California), is a big admirer. He has friends who've eaten there, and they liked it so much they went back a few days later. Even though it serves only one menu, Ishikawa made up a completely different menu just for them.

The restaurant bears the name of its chef, Hideki Ishikawa, which is apt. His take on traditional kaiseki cuisine is so personal that some describe his cooking as "Ishikawa-style." Try his charcoal-grilled black-throat sea perch with Maitake mushrooms or a hot pot of fresh sea urchin and thinly sliced Wagyu beef. Typical of most of our peak dining experiences (and characteristic of many in Tokyo), finding Hideki's hideaway takes some doing. Its menu tells prospective diners, "In case of losing your way, please do not hesitate to call us to escort you." If you do lose your way, it's in a black building behind a fence behind the Bishamon temple. Kagurazaka-Ishikawa.co.jp

AFRICA: THE TASTING ROOM, FRANSCHHOEK, SOUTH AFRICA

"When we look at where we come from, it's opposites," Margot Janse, the Dutch-born chef of The Tasting Room, has said. "Really huge differences. But if we look within those opposites, there are incredible similarities."

Janse was referring to South Africa, but her thoughts apply to the larger world of cuisine. Amid huge differences there are incredible similarities. One similarity is the interest worldwide in making good food that derives from the locality where you are eating it, and Janse's tasting menu, featuring plums and Eugenia flowers from the

restaurant's garden, is all about South Africa and Africa. Three proteins on the menu you don't see everywhere: wildebeest loin, Swartland guinea fowl, roasted Joostenberg duck. Although Janse says she has no signature dish, Larry Olmsted of *Forbes* thinks her small but beautifully precise waffles, made not from batter but foie gras, are "almost too good looking to eat." Also noteworthy: a dessert that arrives inside a sugar shell with hot caramel sauce. Crack open the thin shell with your spoon and house-made coconut sherbet is inside.

The Tasting Room is in a boutique hotel in the Franschhoek Valley, a wine-growing region rimmed by mountains that is inland from Cape Town. (Stellenbosch, another well-known South African wine destination, is nearby.) To quote Janse again: "I don't like bland food. I don't like safe food." Nothing bland about this peak dining experience. Lqf.co.za

EUROPE: LE CALANDRE, SARMEOLA DI RUBANO, ITALY

For us, one of our favorite dishes of all time—and one of the most romantic we know—is risotto. Lemon risotto on its own and with salmon; risotto with chicken and red peppers; carrot risotto from an Italian recipe that turns a lovely orange color; Greek-inspired risotto with lamb and fresh marjoram. They're all pretty much divinely inspired, in our view.

This is why we chose Le Calandre as the peak dining experience in a country and continent devoted to them. Andy Hayler, the food critic and expert on Michelin three-star dining, explains its appeal in words that make our knees go wobbly: "Le Calandre in Italy serves the most perfect saffron risotto, it's just simply the best risotto in the world."

The best risotto in the world? We are *so* there. Although, naturally, you won't find it on some tourist-clogged street in Rome or Venice;

it takes a special effort to get there. It's in a small city in northeast Italy near Padua. Alajmo.it

NORTH AMERICA: THE FRENCH LAUNDRY, YOUNTVILLE, CALIFORNIA

Among many possible choices, says Occam's razor, choose the simplest one. For us the simple choice for North America's peak dining experience is the French Laundry, for the following reasons:

1. It is in the Snob's home region of Napa Valley and the San Francisco Bay Area.
2. It is not in a big city; it takes a bit of an effort to get there—an hour and a half drive from San Francisco, if the traffic isn't too bad.
3. It is on the main street of a historic little wine country town in the center of America's premium wine-growing valley.
4. Across the street from the French Laundry is the three-acre garden where they grow many of the vegetables, fruits, and minigreens they serve in the restaurant. Anyone can walk through it and sit on a bench in the shade and enjoy the scene.
5. On top of his three Michelin stars and multiple citations and awards, Chef Thomas Keller and his book, *The French Laundry Cookbook*, have made a real contribution to the advancement of American cuisine.
6. Keller is a man of modest origins, having been raised by a single mom who managed a restaurant.
7. The food is pretty good, too. Two tasting menus are offered daily; neither uses the same ingredient twice. The chef's menu starts with a classic that remains youthful and fresh, Oysters and Pearls, a sabayon of pearl tapioca with Island Creek oysters and white sturgeon caviar. That's followed by a lineup of Royal Kaluga caviar, roasted carrots and celery salad fresh from the garden, a Hudson Valley moulard duck foie gras pâté, a soft-boiled bantam hen egg with mascarpone-enriched Jimmy Red Corn polenta, grilled Jap-

anese Wagyu, and herb-flavored Elysian Fields farm lamb. Elysian Fields, to the ancient Greeks, was a kind of heaven, and after a meal at the French Laundry that's where you'll feel like you are.

8. Finally, we appreciate balance and symmetry, in a plate of food as in life. *Foodie Snob* began with Keller and the French Laundry and so it ends (almost) with Keller and the French Laundry. Bon appetit!

SNOB ADVICE

All these peak dining experiences are budget-busters, as are so many other fine restaurants. Even the Woodbine Café, if you factor in the price of a cruise ticket to the Falklands and Antarctica, may be the priciest fish-and-chips you will ever have. So what to do about it? Relax. Money expands, contracts, rises, falls. How much or how little you have at any one moment is a temporary and fleeting thing. But a fine meal? Ah, the memories of it can last a lifetime.

FOOD SNOB QUIZ #6
THE INTERNATIONAL KITCHEN

The kitchen is the center of every home and a surprisingly international place. Cooking equipment and appliances hail from countries around the world. This quiz tests how much you know about the global nature of your kitchen and, as with all our quizzes, we proudly include one or two offbeat questions to spice things up. Answers follow the quiz.

1. Wüsthof knives are German-made, which one could easily guess from their Teutonic-sounding name. But it is much harder to discern the country of origin of another fine knife brand. In what country are Global knives made?

   a. Japan

   b. China

   c. Germany

   d. United States

2. For more than a century Steuben exemplified the finest in glassware. Its name also sounds German, but its American founder, Frederick Carder, hailed from a country in the United Kingdom. Which one was it? (By the way, although the company is out of business, Steuben products are still made in association with the Corning Museum of Glass in New York.)

   a. Scotland

   b. Wales

   c. England

   d. Northern Ireland

3. The inventor of that revolutionary kitchen appliance, the Cuisinart, was an American, Carl Sontheimer. But he grew up in a foreign country with a majestic cooking tradition. Name the country.

   a. France

   b. China

   c. Japan

   d. Italy

4. Danish silversmith Georg Jensen founded a company in his own name that makes stylish and highly admired flatware. But in the 1920s his firm was failing until a major showing of his work at an international hotel drew raves and sales, introducing him to a rich new audience. What was the hotel and where was it located?

   a. George V, Paris

   b. Mark Hopkins, San Francisco

   c. Waldorf Astoria, New York

   d. The Savoy, London

5. High-quality stoves are manufactured around the world. Here are five such manufacturers: Elmira, Ilve, Wolf, Lacanche, AGA. Here are their home countries: France, Canada, United States, United Kingdom, Italy. Match the company with its country.

6. Westye Bakke, who founded Sub-Zero refrigerators, worked with architect Frank Lloyd Wright during the Depression, designing custom refrigeration units for his homes. Bakke may have worked on one of Wright's most epic designs, the 1932 Wisconsin home where he lived and that now serves as a campus for his architectural school. Its name?

   a. Fallingwater

   b. Delta Tau Chi

   c. Taliesin

   d. Manderlay

7. The KitchenAid was the first electric stand mixer, introduced to the public just after World War I and invented by engineer Herbert Johnson. As innovative as it was, the KitchenAid was a pricey item for many consumers—two thousand dollars in current dollars—creating an opening for a low-cost mixer that became popular in its own right. Name that mixer, please.

   a. Sunbeam MixMaster

   b. Hamilton Beach KitchenMaster

    c. Betty Crocker Classic

    d. Cheftronic Silver Galaxy

8. "Let there be a place for every article," wrote Elizabeth Ellet in 1857's *The Practical Housekeeper*, "and when not in use let every article be in its place." This is a perfect description for the job of the pantry—derived from a French word, *paneterie,* the "bread room." But Ellet, the daughter of a Revolutionary War captain, made a significant contribution to early American letters. What was it?

    a. Her biography of George Washington is the first major account of an important historical figure written by a woman.

    b. She wrote a major history of the contributions of American women to the Revolution, the first to do so.

    c. She was a friend (and, it is said, lover) of Nathaniel Hawthorne and served as the model for Hester Prynne.

    d. She wrote the nonfiction account of the incidents described in *Uncle Tom's Cabin*, which Harriet Beecher Stowe drew from in her 1852 anti-slavery novel.

9. Fred Waring lived by this wonderful expression, "Let's throw away the rules and have a little genius." An entertainer and big band leader, he showed more than a little genius when, in 1937, he invented the first blender. What was its original marketing slogan?

    a. Big Beat Blender

    b. Cool Crusher

    c. Miracle Mixer

    d. Master Mixer

10. All-Clad is a great American success story. Its founder John Ullam, a gifted metallurgist, developed the idea of sandwiching copper into layers of stainless steel, increasing the heat conductivity of pots and pans. But, in keeping with the internationalization of the

kitchen, a multinational corporation now owns the company and its Pennsylvania mill. Where is Groupe SEB located?

a. Germany

b. Belgium

c. France

d. Russia

Answers: 1. a; 2. c; 3. a; 4. c; 5. Elmira Canada, Ilve Italy, Wolf United States, Lacanche France, AGA United Kingdom; 6. c; 7. a; 8. b; 9. c; 10. c

FOODIE SNOB FINALE

ALPHABET FOR FOODIES

Many years ago Ogden Nash wrote a brilliant piece of nonsense poetry that went like this: "Candy/is dandy/But liquor/is quicker." In the spirit of Nash and other "worsifiers" (his term for versifiers), here is a poem dedicated, affectionately, to foodies everywhere.

A is for Anthony
Stirrin' the pot
That Bourdain
He talks—*a lot.*

B is for Bovine
That's "cow" to you
Where would we be
Without the moo?

C is for the Chef
Who's sorta small
But in his toque
He's six feet tall.

D is for the Diner
And the Jewish deli.
Cheap good eats
That fill the belly.

E is for Escoffier
Frenchman Auguste
For his cooking
We can only lust.

F is for Franey
One hour Pierre
Taught us to cook
With time to spare.

G is for Greens
A joyful ballad
Heirloom tomatoes
Tossed in a salad.

H is for Hamachi
A kind of fish
Have it with sake
It's delish.

I is for Ingredients
Fresh, local,
Seasonable—
Seems reasonable.

J is for James (Beard)
While others roamed
Treasures he found
Here at home.

K is for Knife
Cut, chop, dice
Pare, trim, mince
Split, carve, and slice!

L is for Love Story
We wouldn't fool ya
One for the ages—
Paul and Julia.

M is for Mambo Italiano
Song & cuisine
We'd be lost-a
Without the pasta.

N is for Naan (and)
Tikka masala
Two of the parts
Of an Indian gala.

O is for Oyster
A bivalve fête
Going down smooth
Slippery and wet.

P is for Pie
Peach, pumpkin, berry
Coconut crème
Apple and cherry.

Q is for Q
As in B . . . B . . . Q
Grillin' 'n' chillin'
Yo! Grab a brew.

R is for Rombauer
She went looking
Till she found
The joy of cooking.

S is for Spices
Makin' meals sublime.
Parsley, sage,
Rosemary & thyme.

T is for Tips
How some make rent
Don't squeeze 'em, leave 'em
20 percent.

U is for Utensil
Of course, the fork.
What, no? Chopsticks?
How 'bout a spork?

V is for Vatel
Who took his life
When the fish came late
In went the knife.

W is for Wonton
Chinese dumplin'
Packed with pork
It's really somethin'.

X is for 'Xpensive
As fine dining can be
Don't worry, honey
It's only money.

Y is for Yam
Rhymes with Sam
His favorite dish?
Green eggs and ham.

Z is for Zabaglione
A dessert treat.
All this food talk—
"Please . . . Let's eat!"

ABOUT THE AUTHOR

Kevin Nelson is the author of more than twenty books and a food, wine, and travel writer. Besides *Foodie Snob*, he is also the author of *Running Snob*, another entertaining installment in the Snob book series by Lyons Press. He lives on the doorstep of the Napa Valley and blogs at WineTravelAdventure.com and other sites.